The Finance Liberation

6 Simple Steps to

Fast Financial Freedom

WHILE Living Your Dream Life

Dave Coss

Copyright © 2018 by Dave Coss

All rights reserved. This book or any portion thereof may not be reproduced or used in any manner whatsoever without the express written permission of the publisher except for the use of brief quotations in a book review or scholarly journal.

First Printing: April 2018

The Finance Liberation

Perth, Western Australia 6030

www.financeliberation.com

Ordering Information:

Special discounts are available on quantity purchases by corporations, associations, educators, and others. For details, contact the publisher at the listed email below. Please contact by email info@financeliberation.com.

.

ISBN-13: 978-1718696228

ISBN-10: 1718696221

SPECIAL THANKS

To my loving wife, Kim. Thank you for everything. Without your listening, believing, support and patience, I would never had dared to dream that we would have been where we have been and done what we have done.

I want to thank the people who have helped with the editing of the book.
Rebecca Dew
Kim Coss
Anita Burrows

CONTENTS

	Introduction	9
1	The Finance Liberation Guiding Principles	13
2	Our Personal Finance Liberation Journey	23
3	The Six Steps to The Finance Liberation	37
4	Step 1: Become a Visionary	43
5	Step 2: Stop Being a Consumer	55
6	Step 3: Become a Producer	67
7	Step 4: Become a Marketer	83
8	Step 5: Become an Investor	97
9	Step 6: Become a Giver	123
	Addendum: Save Yourself Rich	137

INTRODUCTION

I'm sure you've seen people driving around in fancy sports cars with their expensive gadgets. You can't help looking as they seem so different. A little jealousy pops up and you think, "Wouldn't it be nice?" Or you go past neighborhoods full of mansions and think, "These people must have it all, right?"

Well, that might not be the case. They could be renting or be in debt up to their eyeballs. You may be surprised to learn that you wouldn't recognize many people as being rich, even if you bumped into them. You might even look at them and think they're poor. They're nondescript and they like it that way.

This book reveals the guiding principles and the six steps of the Finance Liberation model. It also reveals a key concept that has the potential to help you succeed in every area of your life. The steps are simple to understand and implement. But all the steps are powerful and are essential to gaining and keeping wealth.

The Finance Liberation model methodically builds towards financial freedom while minimizing risk. It's a way that anyone can become wealthy. That is a bold statement and comes with some caveats. But I, with hand on my heart, say that anyone can apply the concepts in this book and find themselves wealthy in the not-so-distant future. You will have the tools and methods to maintain your wealth, no matter what life throws at you.

My experience is from the point of view of a married couple. At times only one of us was working, on low wages (sometimes no wages).We have five young children, yet we can still do all we want and have lived in many cities in various countries. So, you don't need to give up on your dreams. In fact, your dreams could drive and inspire you to become wealthy. You might just need a little tweak here and there to set you on the right path. We want to show you how we were able to do that and how you can too.

As a thank you for reading this book and to help you on your wealth journey I would like to give you a gift. Please go to the following page:

www.financeliberation.com/gift

1/ The Finance Liberation Guiding Principles

Being Content

You can't experience true financial freedom if you constantly desire more stuff. By contentment, I don't mean just accepting your lot in life and learning to live with it. Contentment is more of an attitude of satisfaction with your situation. No matter what the situation is, be it extreme poverty or wealth, there isn't the urge to obtain material things. It's a good thing to be content with what you have without the desire to gain more. Of course, taken to the extreme it can mean you don't achieve very much. There's a fine balance between being content and being lazy. We should have the drive to pursue our passions, but we should also be content with what we have.

If you look at many poor people from third world countries you might feel sorry for them, but many of these people seem very happy. I lived in Suva, Fiji for a few months and used to travel by bus (boy was that an experience!). Some rundown city buses had reggae music blaring with a heavy drumbeat.

Like many cities in any country in the world, most people seemed glum. However, just an hour out of Suva, in small towns, most people seemed happy. Why are they happy when they have so little? It's usually because of simple living. Without the stresses of trying to get ahead, and other things that consume their lives, they can enjoy life in its simplicity.

Not having a burning desire for material things can lead to increased enjoyment of life. It's an assumption to think that people who are living simply aren't enjoying life. You don't need to have certain possessions or experiences to be happy. A lot of people enjoy spending money. But you can also enjoy not spending money or saving money (no, it's not a sickness!). Simply saving money isn't going to make you rich. But it can help discipline you in controlling money. You will also develop the bargain hunting skills needed to find investment opportunities.

Using Other People's Money

A reason we've been able to do what we have on such small income has to do with using other people's money. I don't mean stealing, but always, always (yes, I put it there twice) try to get other people to pay for your stuff. I don't mean begging either.

Okay, I'll give you an example. You should get other people to pay for your mortgage. The origins of the word translate to 'death pledge.' We want to have liberation not be tied to something that will suck the life from us. Try to get a property you'll rent out to someone else, so they can pay the mortgage on that property. Or if you buy a house to live in, think about getting boarders in other rooms. Because if you're the one paying the mortgage you're paying after the tax has already come out of your wage. Most people don't take that into consideration.

We had some Chinese student homestays come and live with us not long after we got married. They were in a terrible situation and needed some help. I thought we were coming to their rescue (I am sure we helped a little), but I didn't realize that they would help us financially. The income we received from them helped pay for the mortgage. We had a large house with hardly anything in it. They helped to furnish our house with things that were useful to them and to us.

Many people think it's better to buy than to rent a house. Well, yes, in the long-term it can be, with capital gains and so forth. But you could pay hundreds of thousands more than the sale price in interest, negating any capital gains. If where you live has expensive house prices it might be better to initially rent somewhere cheap or into a boarding situation. That way you can save the majority of your money.

When I use the term, other people's money, you might think about a loan or some other debt. You shouldn't get into debt to buy personal consumer items. One thing that people often get into debt for is purchasing a vehicle. If you can't pay cash for your vehicle you can't afford it and shouldn't get it, unless it's a vehicle you need for work, and in that case, it can be considered a capital investment. There are other options, like buying something cheaper. We used to drive a beat up old van. You could also consider taking public transport or riding a bike. Cycling is great exercise and you'll save so much money on travel expenses.

We find it perplexing that we, with such little income, have done well when others with high incomes struggle. They don't understand this principle. They get things that please them now without thinking about the long-term consequences. Set yourself up to win with leveraging other people's money that they want to give you.

Making Good Return On Investment

I'm going to reveal a key concept that has the potential to help you succeed in every area of your life. I know that's a bold statement. The key is actually a question you ask yourself. You're thinking I am a bit crazy now, right? Okay, the question you need to ask yourself is this: What is my return on investment (ROI)? What do I mean by that? Calculate the ROI for the time, finances, resources, and energies in whatever you do. This question helps cut out negative things in your life that keep you from moving closer to your goals. It's probably best explained by giving some examples.

Example A: Time
Watching a 10-hour DVD series all the way through is not a good use of time, unless it's some sort of documentary that helps you with your work or in your efforts to reach your goals. I'm not saying you shouldn't watch it. But, if you do, you're sacrificing time on one thing to invest in another. Watching the DVD series isn't the issue, the issue is investing so much time in one sitting. And here's the thing: once you compromise the first time, you'll most likely do it again.

Example B: Energy
Anything that uses a lot of your energy for things that aren't healthy for you should be avoided. We only have so much energy in a day and it should be reserved for those things that will give us a good ROI. Teaching your children can take a lot

of energy, but it is necessary for their development. Worrying about something you can't change is something you can do without.

Example C: Finances

Our money has a limited reach and can be easily consumed if we don't take stock of where we spend it. Where we spend money will determine if we're gaining wealth or losing it. Buying your lunch every day, for example, wouldn't generally be considered a good ROI.

ExampleD: Resources

Your things can either be used as consumer items that'll deteriorate to no value over time or for building wealth. The gifts and skills we have can also be used for creating wealth. We should direct our resources toward areas where people have the desire to pay for them.

Asking the question, "What is my ROI?" for every situation might at first seem tedious or overwhelming. But it'll soon become automatic and not take any extra time at all. It can help you eliminate consumerism from your life. This has been one of the key factors in my wife and I becoming wealthy. You have to work hard at it. But, like with anything, if you continue in it for long enough it'll become a habit and it won't be as difficult after that.

Recently, I needed a new computer (don't get me started on my computer issues). Now, what would you do? Would you buy the latest computer you saw so-and-so had? Or would you assess your situation and buy according to what you actually need? Surprisingly (or not surprisingly depending on your position) most people buy technology that's more powerful than they need. They've more features than they'll ever get around to using, so they spend more than they need to.

Well, for my purchase, I didn't get an expensive $2000 laptop computer, but a $400 one. Although we could afford more, the cheaper one was all we needed. Because the computer would mainly be used for business we bought it as a business expense. When you buy a product through a company, you can pay for it before tax is taken out. The sticker price is the same, but when it's a personal expense you pay more because the tax was already removed. If I were to pay for that computer personally it might've cost around 30% more, depending on the tax rate. That can make a huge difference in the true cost to you.

You're always investing into something whether you're working hard or relaxing. You're excluding one thing in order to be able to do another. It's called making opportunity costs. At each juncture, you're deciding what's important at the cost of giving something else up. It happens in every single decision you make.

Earning Passive Income

You're going to struggle to become financially free if you don't have some sort of passive income. Passive investments don't need investor input apart from the decision and initial act of investment. It doesn't mean investors don't spend lots of time worrying about their investments. But they play no active part in making the investment grow or shrink. Some investments take time to manage. However you can pay people to manage it for you to make it more passive.

Early in our marriage my wife and I bought a property for

the purposes of renting it out. It needed more work than we initially thought (I hate it when that happens). We had bought a property a bit larger than the usual size that most people would recommend. It had four bedrooms, which we later converted to six bedrooms and rented it on a room-by-room basis. Every week we would get paid while doing minimal work on the property each year.

By far the most passive investment is putting money into a bank account that earns interest. Some other examples of true passive investments are stocks and bonds. Passive income is worth a multiple of conventional time-based income. That's because you can set up a few passive income investments and replace your conventional income.

You should make it a priority to aim for passive income as soon as you can. It doesn't have to be fully passive. But you should lose the mindset of trading time for money and gain sources of income that aren't tied to your time.

Pursuing Passions

It may seem that pursuing passions is in stark contrast to being content. Being content is being satisfied with what we have. I would define passion as something that'll help you help others. It's very different from just satiating your desires.

Why spend the bulk of your life doing a job you have no passion for? Why would you do what you don't want to do? Actually, that's a silly question. Of course, there are times when you have to do what you don't want to do in order to be able to get where you want to be. Sometimes enjoyment in whatever you do comes down to having the right attitude.

Even though we had the goal of financial freedom, we didn't let that get in the way of us pursuing our passions. We've traveled to various countries to help friends start ministries in their communities. This might not have been the best decision to grow the balance of our bank account. But it was a passion of ours and we were so glad to have done it.

The reason you want to be wealthy is just as important as, if not more so, than the goal of becoming wealthy. You don't want to become a millionaire so you can just sit and stare at your money (well, I hope not). No, you want to become a millionaire to receive all the benefits which money can bring. That could totally be for yourself, like buying cars and homes and poodles. Or it could be for others, like helping the poor, orphans or child sponsorship.

I honestly didn't set out to become a millionaire. I can't really remember whether my motives were selfish or selfless. Let's just say it was selfless to make me feel better. At some point in time, my wife and I looked at our assets, totaled it all up and realized we could retire. We had previously set it as a goal or landmark in our lives, so we could be free to do what we wanted. But we came to understand that we achieved it earlier than expected.

So, should you set out to become a millionaire? I am not sure it's the best idea. Why? Because the goal in and of itself is selfish - to possess a million dollars or have esteem in the eyes of others that you've made your mark. It's better to have a goal amount that you want for financial freedom. How you should calculate that depends on your income and expenses.

I mentioned previously that for many years we were quite happy driving a beat up old van. Why, when we could afford to get a new one? Well, that's all we needed. I didn't really care what people thought of me. If you looked at our spending habits, you might think we were poor. We were very careful with how and when we spent money. Why, when we had plenty to spend how we like? You'll find out in the next chapter where we show our own personal finance liberation journey.

2/ Our Personal Finance Liberation Journey

This chapter is an outline of our personal finance liberation story. Keep in mind that our earnings over many years were below average. While reading this, watch out for the five finance liberation guiding principles mentioned in the previous chapter. We were content with what we had, which helped us save money. We tried to get a good return on investment, that would add value to us rather than distract from the goal. We used other people's money, so we could save our own. We obtained assets that would give us passive income, that worked for us even when we weren't working. And we pursued our passions, which brought enjoyment and fulfillment in our lives. The principles are not explicitly mentioned in this chapter, but they are there. With the right mindset, anyone can do what we have done.

My Work Background (1993-2000)
I worked at a variety of low paying jobs, so I didn't have an illustrious career. I had no thoughts about financial freedom

and just put my money in a savings account. I did learn some life lessons from these jobs, which I will share below.

My first real job was working for my father grooming (cleaning) cars and as a general "gofer" at his car yard. I was getting a pittance of a wage and it wasn't satisfying. But I was working at my own pace and not on an hourly rate, so if I was fast I was paid more. I learned a bit about handling money and the concept of money not being tied to how long you work, but how much you achieve. Later, I changed my hours to part-time, so I could go to university. I studied fixing computers because I thought there was good money in it. I learned that I should do things for the right reasons and not only for making money.

While I was training to become a youth pastor, I worked for a company for a year delivering bakery goods. My day started at five a.m. and finished at nine a.m. It felt great to finish work for the day before many people even started. That work dried up and I became a postie (postman), working at minimum wage. I was surprised to talk to people in the same job who seemed to hate it and wanted to get out. I realized that a positive attitude can make a big difference between enjoying life and just scraping by.

Marriage and Extended Honeymoon (June-Dec 2001)
In June 2001, I married my beautiful wife, Kim. She had part time jobs while she was studying. While at high school she was a supermarket cashier. While at university she worked as a telemarketer and later as a receptionist. Before we got married she had just started a full time job at a consulting company after completing a Master of Business. She wanted to be a mother and decided that she needed to save as much as she could so she could contribute before having children. She

earned more than I did, until she became redundant in her job. The money she brought into the marriage paid for a deposit on our first house. The money I brought in paid for the wedding (why are they so expensive?). We were (and still are) good at saving money. At the same time, others have called us generous toward them.

On the honeymoon, we were told that Kim would have to move to Melbourne for work. After the honeymoon, she went to Melbourne, and I went back to my parent's house. That was a bit weird! We decided that I would give up my job in NZ and live in Melbourne. So I arrived around two weeks later. My wife's company paid for our accommodation. It was a two bedroom apartment in the middle of the Central Business District. They paid her a per diem, which is a daily living allowance. It was the equivalent of the wage I was receiving as a postie. They also offered to fly her back to New Zealand every weekend. Or alternatively, we could both fly back every six weeks. It felt like an extended honeymoon, although Kim still had to work. I didn't find work due to an economic downturn. We didn't know how long Kim's contract would last. We were able to save most of Kim's income because our accommodation was paid for by her company.

First Property Purchase (Dec 2001)

In 2001, we bought our first house at an auction. Kim was in Sydney on business. She had not seen the house, and she was relying on my judgment. My mother had seen the house as well, and Kim trusted her rather than me. There were a few things that had to be completed by the owner before there was a legal title and it took about six months before we could move in. It was dated and needed painting. We did as much work as we could ourselves to make it look presentable. We also tried to save wherever possible on materials.

If I had to point to one thing that set us up to become financially free, it was this property. We initially brought it (as most people do) to live in for ourselves. But as I will elaborate later on in the book, everything you do is an investment. A property purchase should be planned carefully to get the greatest return on investment. We regret not buying more property at that time. There were many bargains around where prices have nearly quadrupled and rents doubled since then. Oh, the joys of hindsight!

Homestay Students (2002-2004)

In 2002, we had the first three of many homestay students live with us. Someone had told us they were being mistreated and we wanted to help them. Initially, we didn't realize hosting them would give us another income source. At that time we didn't even have to pay tax if we had up to three homestays. Although there was effort involved in hosting and we lost some of our privacy, we gained a significant financial benefit. The income received covered our mortgage payments. We also bought items they would need or could use from the profits of having them. For example, we bought beds, tables and heaters that we didn't have before that benefited both them and us. Having homestay students helped us use our house as an investment. The benefits have expanded from that point on.

Second Property Purchase (Oct 2002)

In 2002, we decided to focus on becoming financially free and we bought another house. We didn't have an exact plan, but rental property was how we wanted to get there. We rented out the house furnished to university students. This helped us to make the property cash flow positive, rather than if we rented it as unfurnished.

Living In China (Feb-Dec 2004)
In 2004, after talking with some of our Chinese homestay students, we decided to go to China. We taught at an English training company associated with a church in Guangzhou for six months and enjoyed the whole experience. In order to attract new business, we were asked to give demonstration lessons. Sometimes we would teach entire schools of hundreds of students at a moment's notice. It was crazy, but so much fun. The company paid for our accommodation, which was a 2 bedroom apartment. The wages were low compared to New Zealand, but the cost of living was cheaper. Although we spent all our wages, we saved all the income we received from the properties back in New Zealand.

Near the end of our stay the owner of the English training company asked us if he could gift us the company. We went to China for the cultural experience and didn't anticipate business being a part of our financial freedom journey. However, it seemed like a great opportunity and we decided to do it.

First Property Development (Jan-Mar 2005)
In 2005, we went back to New Zealand for a few months. We converted our house into an upstairs three bedroom unit and a downstairs one bedroom unit. We did a lot of the work ourselves with a huge amount of help from my brother (thanks James!). It took three months to complete and cost around $20,000. By this time we had put the property into a trust. By making this second unit we received two incomes from the property instead of one. Initially this downstairs unit rented for around $800 per month. So, the cost of developing it was covered by the rent in just over two years. We were working on the unit right up to the time we had to rush off to the airport to catch our flights to China.

English Training Business in China (Apr-Dec 2005)
We hadn't had any previous business experience. Here we were, in a foreign country with a language we couldn't speak, running a company we had only limited knowledge about. It was challenging, but a great learning experience.

The company had been losing a lot of money over the years. One reason is they had a prestigious but unprofitable client. So, we made the unpopular decision to discontinue working with them. There were also other clients that didn't renew their contracts with us. Because there was less work we decided we could handle the teaching load on our own. We only retained a manager and a part-time accountant. By making these cuts we took the business from losing money to a breakeven position.

After a few months, we decided it would take money and effort to get the business moving in the right direction. We didn't want to invest our own money into it. So, we gifted back the company to the original owner, and he resold it to another person. We didn't make any money but we learned a lot, which helped us later on in business.

Furniture Importing and Wholesale/Retail Business (2006)
While we were in China, we went to trade fairs that were held in the city of Guangzhou. They hold industry specific trade fairs, and they also have the largest general fair in the world. Anything you can imagine that manufacturers are trying to sell can be found there. We went there to see where all the strange foreigners were going and went back again because of the free food.

We were in awe and hoped that something would jump out at us, something that would sell well in our country. We had tried selling MP3 players, but we had a few issues. The issues were quality control, rapid advances in technology and too much competition. We'd also bought some nifty pens but there wasn't enough demand for them in New Zealand. We tested the market and although we made money, it wasn't enough to make it into a business for us.

In one of the trade fairs, I saw a living room suite that compacted down into small boxes. I looked at the market in New Zealand to see what was being offered by others. I asked my parents if we could store some furniture from China in their garage. It never hurts to have people who will help you out a little bit now and then!

The furniture sold well, so that in a couple of months I went back to China to source more. My parents, understandably, didn't want to continue with this anymore. Their main concern was with the trucks destroying the road. We had to move our "business" somewhere else. We decided that we would move to our first property on the North Shore. We filled up our big double garage, a bedroom and some other space in our house.

Second Property Development (2007)
The next few months were a bit of a blur. We had our first child, Hannah, and also had to move again. The new tenants of our second property were dealing drugs, and we had to get them out. That took six weeks, and we moved ourselves and our furniture over there.

In 2007, we cut a doorway into a large room to make another two bedrooms. We then rented the house on a room-by-room basis. While it provided a higher profit for several years, we found it taxing, so we went back to renting out the whole house to one tenant.

Furniture Business Expansion (2008-2011)

In 2008, an opportunity came up to lease a showroom, warehouse and apartment for a bargain price in West Auckland. The apartment was very basic, and we had to paint it to make it look livable. The two bedrooms actually stretched out over another business. In those parts we had to step quietly as the floor creaked. Sometimes at night the ear piercing alarm of the business underneath would go off and not reset for around ten minutes. There wasn't much point in going to bed early as the late train would shake everything as it roared past every night. They were fun times. We had another two children (Andrew and Jonathan) during the four years we lived there. The accommodation was okay for us and Hannah, but was a little basic for all of us. The price we paid for all that was only USD$1000 per month. You couldn't have rented a small two bedroom house in the same area for that price. We got an amazing deal.

The business did quite well for a couple of years, but then the Global Financial Crisis hit, competition increased and sales went down. In hindsight, we should have sold the business before I lost interest in it. We could've made a nice profit. But sometimes when something is your baby it's hard to let go. I learned you should develop an exit plan as part of your business strategy.

Property Flip (2009)

We wanted to try property flipping. We decided to buy a property, renovate and sell it again. In 2009 we bought a house in Mt Roskill, Auckland. It was only a small one bedroom place, but it had a great view of a park. It took longer than expected (doesn't it always?). After all expenses were paid we only made around $10,000. But here, too, we learned a lot.

Back to China (Jan-Mar 2010)

In 2010, our friends were moving from Guangzhou to Zhuhai. We wanted to visit them and help them with starting a church. We were planning to go with a team, but the rest couldn't get financing. We found out that Kim was three months pregnant and had to make a quick decision to go earlier or not at all. A few weeks later we were off to China with our two eldest children for three months. With the one child policy, many weren't used to seeing a pregnant woman handling multiple children. Kim was frequently told off by concerned grannies. She even climbed a mountain with our 18-month-old Andrew strapped to her. It was worth the effort to go back to China even though it wasn't the best financial decision.

You might wonder how we could afford to travel for three months like this. We had income from our rental properties and bank interest. We only stayed in hotels for a few nights. The rest of the time we rented a furnished apartment in the same complex as our friends. It was only about a quarter of the price of renting in New Zealand. Other living costs were also cheaper. It would be expensive if you went on holiday for only one or two weeks like most people. But living like a local over several months can make it much more affordable. We lived in Zhuhai for three months then headed back to New Zealand.

Software Business (2011-2013)

In 2011, the furniture business wasn't performing well so we began considering other opportunities. I was looking at a place on the internet, the Warrior Forum, for ideas on making money online. I had seen a method someone was using to syndicate all their content with the major social networks in one place. I paid a friend to automate that method. It was a simple piece of software.

Well, I listed this new-fangled software on that same forum and it sold well. We made around US$20,000 from it. It was so simple to make that it seemed a great direction to head in. My friend couldn't help any more, so I hired two coders from the Philippines. It would be ten times the price to hire local employees. We developed other software products to varying degrees of success. But we didn't get the same profit as the first piece of software. It was a good source of income for a couple years.

Financial Freedom (2012)
In 2012, we were told about a new church that would start in Brisbane, Australia. We decided straight away we would go. The landlord decided to triple our rent, so we had to sort out alternative storage for everything before we could set off for our new life in Brisbane. After sorting out alternative storage for everything we set off for our new life in Brisbane. Having lived in very basic accommodation for so long, it was a treat to move into a real house. Nine months after arriving we had our fourth child, Jessica! The Brisbane climate is fabulous, and we thoroughly enjoyed the whole experience. We only meant to go for six months, but we ended up staying for two years.

At this time, we had rent and bank interest coming in as passive income. This meant that we wouldn't have to work while in Brisbane. We also had a very healthy bank balance. We could've retired earlier if we didn't go on so many trips and put our businesses on hold for so long. But I wouldn't have traded those experiences for the world.

In 2014, we went back to New Zealand and lived in the upstairs flat of our first property. As I started putting this book together I was as busy as ever. I was fixing up our properties, writing this book and winding down our furniture and software businesses. It was hard work, but I loved it.

NZ, Fiji, Brisbane, Perth (2015 - 2018)
In 2015, the rental market prices had risen significantly. We decided to reconfigure the layout of the first property to maximize profit. In the upstairs flat, we divided a large living room so the other space could be used for a bedroom. Downstairs we did the same. The space was smaller, like a study, but it made it more desirable. The downstairs alone now returns USD$1100 per month. It's more than what we rented the whole house for ten years earlier.

By 2015, we had paid off the second property, so the rent came directly to us. Nice! While we were living in Fiji, we sold the house near the peak of the market. By simply putting the profit in term deposits, we receive a similar income from interest as we did from rent. That's after all expenses of the property were taken out. It is pretty much stress-free passive income now.

During this time we have divided our time between Fiji, NZ, Brisbane and Perth. We also had another child, Emily. We're chasing the sun, I'm polishing up this book, helping with new and newish churches, revisiting past friends and making new ones. Loving it!

Can You Do It?

As you can see, we're not like most people. We feel as though we're ordinary people who have been privileged to do some extraordinary things. I guess we have done things that most people wouldn't do, but in terms of our wages, we were average (or below average). We only had a double income for around one year of our marriage. In fact, there were quite a few times where we weren't earning any wages at all.

You can retire when your passive income exceeds your expenses. If you live where expenses like rent and food are cheap, then it's easier than in more expensive cities. When we move to places where the cost of living is cheaper, we use this as a saving period. In more expensive places, we might not grow our finances as much or choose to stay as long. Ideally, you want to be mortgage free on the property that you live in. Or have a rental property which will give you income to offset the rent where you stay. Then, you can live anywhere you want.

It wasn't until we took stock of our situation that we realized we could afford to retire. We have income coming in every week that far exceeds our needs. We've achieved financial freedom by saving, investing, business, redeveloping property and minimizing expenses. I'll refer to examples later to show you how some decisions made us wealthy and others did not do so well. We made many mistakes along the way and certainly could've done it quicker. That's right, not everything we've done has turned to gold. You can be wealthy in a few short years, by tweaking what you do with your money and following the simple steps of the finance liberation model.

3/ The Six Steps to The Finance Liberation

When contemplating how we became financially free (and observing others), I concluded that it's actually quite a simple process. There are other ways to do it. But most require lots of energy, luck and generally make you do things you don't want to. Below is an introduction to the steps that I believe are the most sure-fire way to become financially free (with a more in-depth explanation in the chapters to follow). I also give a real life example for each of the steps.

Step 1: Become a Visionary

This is where you should start. It helps to find your real motivation for doing things and sets your course. It becomes your blueprint for your life. You need to figure out what you are supposed to do and aim to do it.

I was sitting on this cool cocoon-shaped chair that we had bought for our furniture company. I wasn't thinking about much, as guys tend to do. Anyway, this thought came to mind that in 2012, we would be financially free and able to help start churches. Initially, it wasn't a very inspiring thought. But as I began to mull it over it felt like all the puzzle pieces of my life were coming together. We had helped in starting churches in different countries and we wanted to travel to help again. I previously had a vision where I saw our luggage all packed up ready to go. It seemed to mean we were going to be living our lives out of suitcases.

It was going to be difficult because we had a furniture company which had a fixed location. My interest in the company had already waned. It was during the global financial crisis and sales were down. I began to think of ideas that could help with the vision.

Step 2: Stop Being a Consumer

A consumer mentality is like a cancer that's out to ravage you. Most people don't realize how insidious this is. They're consumed with things that distract from achieving anything of lasting significance. Dealing with consumerism clears the ground to set your foundation. Without doing this, whatever you build could crumble.

Before I had the vision, I wasn't in a great place in regards to my thinking. I would go to work but I wasn't exactly working. I should've been trying to sell furniture. Sometimes there wasn't much to do, but instead of trying to drive the business forward I would waste time. I would often be checking sports scores and consuming news. I was also buying lots of ebooks, hoping to get some money making inspiration. I was doing a lot of research and not doing any work. I needed to realize that it was a destructive path that I was on. Having a vision before me helped me to deal with this issue.

Step 3: Become a Producer

Add value by producing things that people actually want. Not what you want, but what people will be happy to pay you for.

I was looking for other opportunities and came across an internet marketing forum. I bought an ebook there that mentioned a website that helped with promotion of your website and social media. I thought it was a good idea to make software that could link your website with this other website. I knew it was something that I could use myself, and similar products on that forum sold well. I asked a friend how long it would take to put the software idea together. He told me it would take a maximum of three days. Well, three weeks later he finally got it finished!

I started to worry that this particular software didn't look great. I mean it did the job and everything, but I was expecting it to look nice. I remembered reading that sometimes 80% is good enough and if I aimed for perfection I might never sell it. So, I decided that I would sell the software warts and all. In the end, it sold better than anticipated. One of the reasons was there was a hungry market for it.

Step 4: Become a Marketer

Learn how to sell. Marketing is influencing people to take action. This is one of the most important skills you can gain. Being able to persuade people to part with their money will make you rich.

The software was finished, now I had to do something more important. I had to write the marketing sales letter. I hadn't had much experience in writing a sales letter. I looked at many others to see if I could get some inspiration and model mine after something good. There were many but they all seemed a bit over-hyped and boring. I decided I would try to write from scratch. I wrote with self-deprecating humor and was very honest. This was different from the hype of most sales letters, so it could've been a total failure. The sales page wasn't pretty at all. It was simply words on a page. Actually, let's be honest, it was ugly. I found my own style of writing which I enjoyed putting together and accomplished what I set out to do. When people read the sales letter they were entertained and could see the value of the product.

Step 5: Become an Investor

Whatever we do we are always investing our time, energy, resources and finances into something. To gain financial freedom you should invest your money to make it work for you.

After my initial success with releasing the software, my friend couldn't help anymore. So I had to look for more software developers to help me. I invested in maintaining and developing more software. I also paid for other things that helped make this into a real business. I poured more time into this new endeavor than I did with the furniture business.

Step 6: Become a Giver

Give and it shall be given to you. Literally, this happens. It's not a nice jingle to make people feel good or coerce them to give. Our motivation to give should not be influenced by a desire to get back. Yet giving is one of the most effective ways to gain much more than you originally had. It's a mysterious money multiplier.

I had quite a few issues with the software launch to begin with. It was mainly small technical ones. I found that in being honest, patient and helpful in sorting out the issues, most people were grateful. They would, in turn, help others and would also promote my product. As I had a reasonably successful product launch, it got me noticed. I had other product creators wanting to work with me. I was paid for promoting some other people's products. I also found that those people wanted to promote my products when I released other software.

Another Example

We could also use the analogy of a real estate developer for these steps. You have someone who visualizes the purpose and the design of the buildings. You then set about clearing the site and establishing the foundations. They construct the buildings. The buildings will need to be sold. The developer can then invest that money into other projects. They would beautify the area with parks and community facilities. It makes it a nice area to live thereby increasing the potential profit. It would be a sense of pride for the developer to see a beautiful area rather than a slum. And it would serve as a testimony to the work they could produce. So pleased local authorities would give future projects to them rather than to others who are unproven. They've created something that didn't exist before that'll continue to serve generations.

Those are the steps in a nutshell. The following chapters go into more depth and provide examples of the steps in action.

4/ STEP ONE: BECOME A VISIONARY

"The two most important days in your life are the day you were born and the day you find out why."

Mark Twain

What lights your fire? What gets you up in the morning excited about the day? Having a vision for your life is like setting up a blueprint to give you guidance for the future ahead. You might not have all the details sorted, but it helps you to focus on important things when you get distracted. If you don't have a vision for your life, you'll struggle to have enough energy to push through when it gets hard. Some people go as far as having a personal vision and mission statement for themselves. It's not a bad idea at all to write it down.

Your vision should be achievable. You might see yourself as the President of the United States, but if you're not born in the U.S.A, then it won't happen. Or maybe that space station on Mars floats your boat (or starship). Having said that it must be achievable, it might not be achievable by us, but we could help someone else achieve it. It should be bigger than you can handle right now. Some visions are completed by succeeding generations, so you might only achieve a part of it.

Your vision shouldn't be just about yourself, but it should aim to help others as well. I can see some people shaking their heads at this point. Why is this in a money book? "Just give me the money!" Whoa there, Nellie! So, when you get your money, what then? Spend it on your desires? Then get more money to spend it on even more desires? You see, money and the things money can buy, don't fulfill. There are many rich and famous people who seem to have it all yet they're unfulfilled.

The money you crave to give you the freedom you desire is empty. Don't get me wrong, the freedom money can bring is great. I love being able to do what I want and go where I want at any time. But if that's all I do, then it's worthless. I've missed my point in life. We're meant to do things beyond just thinking about ourselves. What do you want to do? For me, it's helping people with finance and starting ministries around the world. For others, it could be helping out at a rest home or trying to free child slaves or mentoring youth.

I can remember a story I heard about a woman who told a counsellor she was unhappy and lacking a sense of purpose. His answer was to go serve the homeless. She did that and miraculously she found that her depression was gone. It wasn't a miracle that she found purpose in helping others.

How to Achieve Your Vision

1. You Have to Believe that You Have a Purpose to Fulfil

You should believe you have a purpose to fulfil. Do we have a purpose or are we only products of chance? As a Christian, I firmly believe we're designed for a purpose. Now we could debate about whether you believe in God or have evolved from a common ancestor. I won't do that here. Even if you don't think that you were designed, I want you to consider that you have unique gifts and abilities. These can make a difference in the world if you'll embrace them.

There are many great resources you can use to find out the gifts you have, so you can build on your strengths. Now these are good, but they're not your purpose. They are skills that can help you to achieve it. If you don't set aside time to think about what your purpose is then you'll end up just going through the motions. Not that you won't be successful. But even if you're successful in something that doesn't mean you have led a fulfilling life.

It's interesting to listen to the research on people as they're close to death and the regrets they have. They mostly mention not spending more time with friends and family. Working too much and worrying what others would say about their dreams are two others. This is a great reality check. Do we want to get to the end of our lives and have things left undone? We might feel that our lives have come to nought and have a great sense of regret, even if we succeeded in the eyes of everyone else. No one knows how that regret will feel, but I am sure it will hurt deeply. I can think of times that I look back in regret on some things and the pain associated can be quite a burden. However, there is nothing we can do about the past. Sometimes negative experiences help motivate us to make the most of current opportunities.

There have been things that my wife and I have done that were not the best financial decision. But it was part of what our purpose was, so the sacrifice we made was worth it. If you can make the trade to give away something to achieve your purpose, go for it. It'll cost you, it always does, but it's worth it. Let me give you an example. We had a furniture business. It was not running that well because of the economy and a lack of focus on my part. We decided that we would move from Auckland to Brisbane, Australia to help start a new church. We had a lot to do. We had to sort out our furniture business, cease trading and store the furniture somewhere. We had to pack up our apartment and find a place to rent over in Brisbane. There were significant costs associated with this move. It made no financial sense. But it was part of our purpose and we were happy to make the trade. Would I do it again? Yes, yes and yes!

This may seem strange in a book about financial freedom and it somewhat is. I don't mean spend on everything you desire or make foolish financial decisions, even if you think it's fulfilling your purpose. In our situation, we were already quite wealthy. If you are not at that stage, then you might have to curb your enthusiasm a bit. I know some people who will fly halfway across the world for these "worthy" causes even while in debt. In general, I wouldn't think this is a great idea. If you're in debt you should focus on getting rid of that. Don't go further into debt even for a "worthy" cause. It will delay your financial goals and your ability to help in greater measure in the future. I give examples later in the book about making money work for you while you are fulfilling your purpose. Yes, it can work in some situations.

2. You Have to See It Before You Receive It

You have to see your vision in your mind's eye. I mean actually envision it. See yourself in that situation doing what you believe you are supposed to do. Vision is very powerful. I can think of the businesses we had and I saw them all before they were a reality. For example, our furniture business. I saw us selling furniture and making money. I actually saw it. It wasn't clear or in technicolor, but it was in my mind's eye and I saw the furniture we were selling. Now, it might not have worked out exactly as I saw it, but it was close enough. The vision I saw was enough to motivate me to make it a reality. There will be things you see that'll turn out as you see them. That's the power of vision.

If you can see it, you can have it. Disneyworld in Florida, opened five years after the death of its creator, Walt Disney. Someone asked Mike Vance, the Creative Director of Disney Studios, "Isn't it too bad Walt didn't live to see this?" Vance replied, "He did see it - that's why it's here."

If you can't see it, it won't happen. If you dream about something but just see it as a dream that's too difficult, then it won't happen. You need to imagine yourself achieving your vision, to put aside all distractions. We're not talking about seeing yourself eating ice cream and then getting some from the freezer. That is not a vision, that is meeting a desire.

Your vision is like constructing a blueprint for the completed design. It's like you're putting together a design plan for your purpose as you think and plan what your next steps are. Focus in on your vision and your seed thoughts will build it out. It will become more detailed and reveal some of the steps involved. The clearer you can see it the better. This will give you a picture or snapshot of your vision in your mind. You'll have it appear from time to time to keep you motivated. Thoughts are like seeds, which become ideas. Ideas become plans and plans become actions.

You will, of course, have to do some work. But the vision before you will drive you on to achieving it. I remember when we were struggling to get our internet marketing "business" up and going. It was hard work, and we didn't seem to make progress. I had a vision of us doing what we wanted, that is starting churches, and it was all I needed. My energy levels rose. I had focus, I had passion.

What you envision doesn't always turn out to be what you expected. Even if you're going in the right direction things won't always go according to plan. Sometimes it can be because you're focusing on that which you're not meant to do, or it can be for several other reasons. But don't get discouraged, this will happen, and it's part of your journey.

You'll always make time for those things which you deem as important. Take the time to daydream. Some people might mock you for this as it might seem like something a child may do. It could look like it's not very productive. But you can't get a vision if you don't take the time to see it. It's the seed of an idea that grows to fruition. It's easy to spend our spare time wasting it in things that aren't productive. If you set aside time for daydreaming, then you'll find it'll help you to focus on what you want to do. I am not talking about daydreaming that's away with the fairies and not grounded in reality. You should also control your thoughts so you don't get carried away into something fruitless or destructive.

This isn't a one-time event. You have to continue to keep the vision before you and think about it often. You should dream about it when you have the time and plan for commencing and completing it. Your passion will help you push to achieve it quicker than you could without that motivation. It'll make you focus on it for longer and more concentrated periods. If you don't do this, you'll lose it. Sure the vision might come back from time to time. Keeping the vision before you will keep you motivated to achieve it. Give it your time and energy and eventually you'll be rewarded by the goal achieved.

3. You Have to Believe You Will Receive Everything You Need to Achieve It

Your vision should be much bigger than you can handle at this moment in time. If you focus on your vision, you'll find you'll attract those things you need to achieve it, be it people, resources, finance or what have you. That doesn't mean you can simply think about those things and they'll come to you. You actually have to do the work needed.

With this book you are reading here, I didn't tell too many people about it. I only told some people as it was coming together and because they specifically asked what we were up to. I hadn't written a book before. I struggled to write anything of great length. I like writing bullet points, but that didn't stop me, because I believed I had something of real value to give. I wanted to share it with as many people as I could. The strange thing is as I thought about it, the ideas flowed and I found myself writing better than ever. As it has come together, people offered to proofread, edit, design covers and promote the book. All of that for free!

Sometimes we disqualify ourselves because we feel inadequate. Don't disqualify yourself, put yourself in contention by doing it. Others might try to disqualify you and tear you down, you don't need to do it as well. I didn't feel I had the ability to write this book. But I've somehow come up with the ability to do it through passion and experience of the things I am writing about. You'll find that too when you are about to set off on that journey into the unknown of pursuing your passions. Somehow you'll find that you can do things you didn't think you had the ability to do, though it might be a little limited. I can't describe to you how satisfying and fulfilling that is.

I recently heard about a family friend that has an amazing vision. He was a successful engineer. He had a dream to revolutionize waste processing to make useful products and end up with near zero waste. It also has a community transformation plan to go with it. It's the most ambitious plan I've heard of with billions of dollars needed to build this dream. He has somehow raised this money to start the process! Some are investing for the potential profit, but for others it's about the community transformation. They believe in the vision and have devoted their lives to it. Oh, by the way, he is in his eighties!

So, you'll find that as you strive for your vision you'll receive what you need to achieve it, be it abilities you didn't think you had, finances you need or people to come on board with your vision. Whatever it is you need will come.

4. You Have to Fight for It

Oh yes, that's right, you have to fight. You didn't think it would be easy did you? Anything of value is worth fighting for. Your fulfilled vision doesn't arrive suddenly one day, as if you are walking down the road and stumble over it. No, it comes only after a series of tests. There are things in our lives, even our own thoughts, that aren't compatible with our vision. We have to go through these tests to eliminate some of these "pests" and also to equip us for the journey ahead. Now at the time, we may not recognize the tests. They may seem like unreasonable road bumps that are a waste of time and effort. But they're essential to making us who we're supposed to become. The journey is important.

You'll get people telling you it can't be done, you shouldn't try, it's been tried before, or it's too difficult. They'll look at you funny or change the subject. You know how it is. We assume that people will celebrate our marvelous plans and generally they don't. They might give you a look as if they've heard it all before (maybe they have). You can tell if people want to hear about it. Sometimes it's better to share with people who are interested and you believe will spur you on.

Here's what I do, I hardly ever talk about my dreams and plans with people unless they press me. I'll then briefly touch on something I've planned and am passionate about and give them a preview. If they ask no more questions, I'm finished. I used to become upset they didn't "get it," so I would carry on some more. Most people don't care for ideas, they want to see results. So move on. Otherwise, you'll get discouraged. Actually, some people will share with anyone they can to seemingly get advice. Or they share their dream with people to boast as if they've already done it. Oftentimes they're afraid to pursue their dreams and want people to help them. If they don't get any takers, it will deflate their dream. They lose momentum and ultimately give up. It's best to just go do it and don't say anything until you're done. People will understand your vision once you've accomplished it, not before. What you've done will speak for itself and others will speak about you.

We often have people say how surprised and inspired they are by what we're doing. I had previously tried to explain to someone a few times over a few years what we wanted to do, but he never got it. In reality, I know I probably didn't communicate very well. This had been frustrating because I so wanted him to understand. He would suggest things he thought would help but were totally in a different direction. He now understands better and is excited for us.

We helped with a new church being established. I talked to the leader about how he seemed to pass me over when finding someone to bring a teaching to the members. He said that not everyone can teach, and it's a special gift. I believe it was because I am a bit of an introvert. I know how uncomfortable it can be watching someone struggle in getting the words out. You feel for them. However, I like to prove people wrong and don't like to be put into a box. I asked for him to reconsider and he reluctantly gave in.

The time was approaching, and I was getting quite nervous. Now voices in my head were saying I was going to make a fool of myself. Anyway, I finally gave this message and it went better than I expected. The leader said it was outstanding and he was surprised. I wasn't all that surprised because I believed I could do it and desired to do it. Now I have done it, I don't desire it so much (if at all), but it has helped me to grow in this area. Looking back, maybe I should have insisted a lot earlier. That could've been my last chance. It can feel like someone saying, "This is your lane, you run there and that's all." Well, don't settle for that. I'm not saying to be an upstart and demand things and not to be submissive. We all need to be team players for an organization to run effectively. But don't let people limit you to a box you weren't designed to fill.

There will be others that oppose what you do or are the competition. They can make the journey harder, but the battle can make you stronger. Sometimes your gifts won't be appreciated or you might not get the position you think you deserve. You shouldn't fear competition; you should embrace it. In fact, encourage those who might seem in competition with you.

You'll find it tough. If you don't, obviously your dream isn't big enough. Because it should challenge your socks off. You should grow in areas of your life that you thought previously impossible. Once you're walking out your vision, it'll become clearer. It may even seem to be bigger. Your capacity to handle what is thrown at you will need to become larger. Anything is possible to those who will fight for their dreams.

If you still have no idea about your vision, find someone else who has an amazing vision and help them to achieve their goals. In helping someone else achieve their vision you might discover yours. You might find your vision and people to help you achieve it.

5/ Step Two: Stop Being a Consumer

Who is a Consumer?

For the purposes of this book, I have given the following definition:

A consumer is someone who is self-absorbed and will act according to wants rather than needs.

Consumers Make Decisions by Emotion Rather than Reason

Consumers are lead by the question of, "How does it make me feel?" rather than what is best for the situation. They're driven by their desires and have an entitlement mentality. Consumers usually don't achieve anything of great significance. That's because by nature consumers think about themselves too much. They may do things that they consider good. But it's for their desire to be affirmed as good rather than doing something good because it's a good thing to do.

We're all consumers to some extent, but many people are characterized by this trait.

Consumers Will take Short-Term Pleasures over Present time Sacrifice for Long Term Gain

There's a famous experiment where they offer children a marshmallow. They tell them that they can eat the marshmallow now or they can wait a period of time and they'll get another one. You can imagine their little minds racing at the excruciating process of figuring out the best option. Some immediately stick it in their mouths and gulp it down. That way they don't have to experience the decision making pain.

At the root of a consumer is the desire to please one's self. Now, we all suffer from this in our lives. We think about ourselves first and if they're lucky, we might think of other people. A consumer doesn't necessarily care what is happening in the world around them. They will think short term. For example, voting for a system that gives them immediate benefits while short changing future generations.

They think buying material things will fulfill their desires and then they'll be happy. They may compare themselves to others and think they'll feel special in possessing these things. They almost can't resist the temptation presented to them. Sure there might be enjoyment in those things for a time, but it doesn't satisfy long term and brings no real fulfillment. I'm sure you know someone like this and you might have some areas of your life that are ruled by consumerism.

Magical, Manipulative Marketing

You've seen the glitzy billboards or the cool TV ads where if you buy such-and-such you will become: sexy, smart, cool, rich and liked. Okay, the ads don't say that, but that's what they're implying. Some companies spend millions of dollars on their message to persuade you to buy.

And marketing works. Why else do they spend all this money? Because they know a certain amount of people will buy. This isn't about educating you to make informed decisions. It's about hitting emotional triggers in the audience to make them feel a certain way. These companies are feeding the consumer inside you. They target those things that make the consumer do what they do best, that is to focus on their own desires and to be selfish. Most people don't realize that they've been under the spell of these companies. They've fallen for the message that the companies want them to believe. We've all been sucked in, but have the ability to break free from the spell. You don't have to be deceived unless you really want to.

Let me give you an example: Apple products. I could show you that a particular Apple device isn't the best in its range. We could compare specifications and pricing against some of their competitors. But if you've fallen under the spell of the marketing machine, I would be powerless to stop you from purchasing. If these companies make seemingly inferior products, yet charge more, how do they get away with it? They make their products good enough. I'll get many people hating me now because I used Apple as an example.

Expectation

Expectations are set for us at different stages of our lives. If something is consistently done the same then we always expect it that way. Otherwise, it feels wrong. You might also have a sense of being overlooked if you expect to be treated a certain way and do not receive it.

We used to take our children to McDonald's about once a month. We would buy them a 50 cent ice cream and then they would get to play on the playground. This was very cheap, but it was still a treat and they were grateful for it. Did they look longingly at others kids getting a happy meal? No. They were content with what they were given. Had we, like others we saw, purchased a happy meal for them, every time we went there they would expect to get a happy meal. I know this because every time we went there or even close to one, we would get questions like, "Are we going to McDonald's and are we going to get an ice cream?" It was never for anything else because they never experienced anything else from us. They had received some nice goodies from their grandparents, and expected it every time from them, but not from us. If we started out like that they would expect it every time. It wouldn't be a treat for them and they wouldn't be grateful. This is a big problem where people expect to get something and don't feel grateful for what they receive.

In the same way, you can train yourself to expect less than you want and be grateful for what you get. When you receive more than what you anticipated you are grateful. Life seems more enjoyable. We went out to a dinner with some friends that cost more than we would spend over an extended period of time. We enjoyed it so much as it was different to what we would normally have, and we were grateful for the experience. We could tell with others it was a bit ho-hum as if it was a normal experience for them. If you've no expectations then you'll be pleasantly surprised when something "nice" happens to you. In fact, you'll find that "nice" things happen to you often.

Entitlement

Expectation then leads on to a sense of entitlement, the feeling of deserving something. We live in an age of the entitlement or "I deserve it" mentality. People want to reward themselves for being them (Oh how nice!). They think that they deserve to buy lunch every day or deserve to go to the movies whenever they feel like it. Or they deserve the latest gadgets when they come out. Some people believe they're entitled to whatever anyone else has. "If they have it, why shouldn't I?" This kind of mentality is self-defeating because it focuses on unimportant things. It puts your desires ahead of your destiny.

I knew a leader who felt entitled to receive a certain salary. He decided to give it to himself because he controlled the finances. He made decisions with an organization's money that benefited himself. Everyone else thought that it was extreme and not justified considering the circumstances. Needless to say this didn't work out very well. Thankfully the leader left. He was a drain on the organization. It couldn't grow from that kind of leadership, especially financially.

It's not necessarily the rich or successful that feel a sense of entitlement. Those who are poor, abused, or undervalued can feel entitled to be bitter. A sense of entitlement in any sphere is going to cause trouble. It can land you in financial strife. I know people who think that they deserved a certain type and year of car because they earned it. This car was the ruin of them because they got a loan and couldn't afford the repayments.

Because . . . If you use this word after whatever you decide that you're entitled to, then you can justify anything you want. Try it. I need this iPhone because it'll help me in my studies. I need this car because it'll help me to get to work and I won't have to worry about maintenance. I need this jacket because I look good in it. I need this computer because of potato. You can stick anything after that word and you have justified your entitlement. Get rid of your need and 'because' words. If you don't need it, then it's just a want. Although we shouldn't quench all our desires, you need to have them under control.

Wants vs Needs

How do people get this mixed up? A need is something you have to have to survive. Things like clothing, shelter, food and water. Even in those things, you can go to extremes in living beyond your means. Wants are things you don't need; they're your desires. A smartphone is not a need; it's a want. You may need it for business, but you don't need it for school. Same with a computer or a car. A TV is a want. Yes, that's right. It would be good to go through a list of the things you have and see if they're wants or needs.

How to Deal with the Consumer

You might need to dig down deep and get rid of any consumerism that is lurking. Recently a house was built next door to us. They took away truckloads of dirt to make a level foundation on which to build. The foundation part of the building took a couple of months to complete. The rest of the building went up quite quickly in comparison. If the building was built without a proper foundation, then it would be unstable and collapse. So, it is with our lives, if it's built on consumerism.

You've seen those people who seem to have it all. They look to be doing well financially because they make large incomes. But many of these people are ripe candidates for losing everything. Why? In flaunting their wealth, they show that they've built their lives on the foundation of consumerism. This is something that is insatiable and unstable. They leave themselves open to many issues that can come against them. The whole house of cards will eventually come tumbling down. Regularly, you'll see newspaper articles of people who had millions, but are now bankrupt. Sure, some of these people will bounce back. But if they do make it, it'll be because they've realized their failures, and rectified their mistakes.

If you have a problem, you need to deal with the root of the problem. Otherwise, the problem returns because it hadn't been uprooted and was allowed to grow back. If you need to buy a coffee and a doughnut each day to help you feel "right", then there's an issue you need to deal with. I will reward myself with a small celebration after achieving something of significance. It certainly is not everyday that I do that. If you have to reward yourself everyday, that is called an addiction.

Don't think that you can compromise with this in just getting one thing you desire. For example, you have seen the latest tech gadget and you have to have this one thing. The problem is if you give into your desire here, you'll tend to compromise on something else in the future. You're deceiving yourself to think that you're not a consumer when something here has shown that you are.

Sacrifice

If you want to get ahead, you'll have to make sacrifices. What is a sacrifice? It's giving up a comfort or a lifestyle you enjoy because it hinders you from achieving your goal. Now, sacrifices can be quite hard to make at the beginning. There might be a sense of loss. But after awhile, you get used to living without these things. You now have more free time to devote to those things you deem as important to achieving your goal.

Many people think that those who are rich spend money on their pleasures with what they earn, but that's not the case. They don't spend from what they earn, they spend out of their overflow. That's something we will touch on later. Many people who are poor get into debt to buy things like huge TVs. This actually keeps them in poverty because they get caught up in what they think will make them happy. They don't do the things that'll get them out of their situation.

We've made many sacrifices in our lives. But to us, they've not seemed like sacrifices, because we've seen the end goal. Any sacrifice we put ourselves through, we endured because we knew what was important. Like I said, you get used to the lifestyle you lead. We could've easily bought that nice car or those gadgets. We had the money and more, but doing that would set us back further from achieving the goal.

People told us we were crazy to live in a warehouse. We had a showroom for our furniture and a warehouse out back. Above the warehouse, there was an apartment. I use the term apartment loosely as it was very basic. We lived there for over four years. Two of our now five children were born while we lived there. Some people said that it wasn't a good environment to raise kids with no lawn for them to play on.

We considered the concerns of people because we wanted the best for our children. Then we realized in the city we were living in, there were only three months of the year you could play on a lawn anyway! It would've set us back a couple of years to take that advice. Sometimes those who love you don't see what you see. So you have to consider what they say and do what's best for you. My not taking their advice hasn't affected our relationship. Sure they weren't happy at the time. But now that the situation has passed, they don't need to give us advice about that particular thing.

We lived in the warehouse not because we couldn't afford other places but because we saw the vision ahead. We sacrificed the little in the present to get more in the future. We only planned to stay there for perhaps six months. But we understood the benefits of staying longer and realized it wasn't much of a sacrifice, even though people thought we were mad to live there with our expanding family! The children all survived, and when we moved to a 'real house', they were excited and didn't take it for granted. In the long run, they'll have very few memories of the warehouse - good or bad. We saved so much by living there that it fast-tracked our savings. It helped us to get where we are now, retired, doing what we want to do.

You may think you don't want to sacrifice. Well tough. You'll have to sacrifice somewhere along the way. Trust me, if you want to be rich you'll make sacrifices. Those who sacrifice understand that temporary present comforts can bring future discomforts. But, temporary discomforts will bring future comforts. Those future comforts generally have greater satisfaction and longevity.

Delayed Gratification

We would all like to get the latest electronic goods now, but we can't afford them all. I wanted to update my phone (notice I said wanted not needed). Ok, my phone was pretty old, and I decided it would be a good idea to get a "smart phone" because (arrrgh, there's that word again!) it would help in business as well. So, I did a little research into what things I wanted and then looked for secondhand sets. I got one that was almost new for around a tenth of the price of when it had first come out. In the end, I got what I wanted. It's just that I got it a year or so after I originally wanted it. Ask yourself why you want it now when you can have it later at a fraction of the price. You may even find at a later time you don't actually want it. Think of the money you could save.

Many people buy homes for themselves too early in their journey. If they delayed their purchase they could achieve financial freedom earlier. When buying a house most people don't consider it as an investment, but like it's their personal retreat. They pour money into a property that brings about little financial ROI. Generally, when something is bought as a consumer choice, it's a bad financial choice. What if something happens and they need to move? They may need to rent the house or sell. These kinds of homes that people have don't usually get a good rental return. If they need to sell they could be subject to the whims of the property market cycle. Of course, capital gains can help, but it's not guaranteed. This can set back retirement by decades because of thinking like a consumer.

Don't Judge a Book by Its Cover

Some people would look at us and might think we're poor, or at least not wealthy. We're very different from most people we know, not necessarily regarding personality or outlook on life, but how we handle money. You see, just because I am wealthy doesn't mean I have to go around acting as if I can afford anything I want. Money is a factor in what we choose and we enjoy saving money.

I usually take some time to make sure I get a bargain. For example, I was looking to buy some new tyres for our car. Finally, after a few online searches, I bought the tyres at the best price possible with some extras thrown in. Some might see it as a waste of time and just buy the first thing that fits. It's not a bad idea if you are cash rich and time poor. I have the time and enjoy the hunt. Having a habit of bargain-hunting can help when looking at big ticket purchases or potential investments. See most people buy what feels right. Bargain hunters have to get a bargain. Having the habit of saving money can be powerful to boosting your bank account balance.

Sometimes saving money can have added benefits in other areas. For example, I needed to get to a meeting from one area of Suva, Fiji to another. It would take about 15 minutes in a taxi and cost around $8. Most people who could afford it would take that option. But, because I planned it and have the time, I would usually take a bus part of the way (70 cents) and walk the rest (30 minutes). It took a total of around 40 minutes. I saved money but also got the added benefit of good exercise. It was a two for one deal. Some people pay for expensive gyms, and have to travel and take time out of their schedule to get there.

Some might see this as stingy or cheap, but if you're not spending on yourself that's sacrificial. It's when you're withholding from others where it can be considered stingy. Not being a consumer has been a very successful strategy for us. Maybe being a consumer is the one thing that is holding you back from achieving your dreams.

6/ Step Three: Become a Producer

Producers are those with vision and passion that deliver value to the marketplace. Keeping the vision in the forefront of your mind stirs up passion. Passion keeps you motivated to fulfil your purpose. In your journey in life, you'll gain skills that become valuable to others.

Producers have Vision and Passion

Vision will keep you focused. You shouldn't change your game plan from one month to the next. You can't become successful if you're only trying something out. That is a recipe for mediocrity. You need to focus for long enough to at least get the job done. Entrepreneurs are notoriously bad at finishing something. Many enter the market without understanding the costs and run out of money. They may be amazing at starting things, but they need to follow through to the end to achieve success. See it before you produce it. You'll then understand you need to add value to the marketplace to attract wealth.

Many of the best chefs in the world are the best because they devote themselves to the task often to the detriment of other things. Some are so passionate about their creations that they don't live a very balanced life. Now, I believe it's important to have that balance and you can. But if you want to achieve success, sacrifices are necessary to achieve what you want. Otherwise, you obviously don't want it enough.

Producers Add Value

Although it's important for you to have a vision and a passion, unfortunately no one wants to pay you for that. Sorry to burst your bubble. What do you have that people are willing to pay for? People are quite happy to pay others if they feel they're getting value. What is of great value to one person could hold little or no value to another person. All your potential customers or employers are looking to see if you can add value and how much you can add. If they can't see it, then it's highly unlikely they'll want what you offer. You may have what you consider a lot of value, but if people don't want what you offer then it doesn't matter. You need to match your value with what the market wants.

It surprises me what some students study at university. I went to a fine art display at a prestigious art school in Auckland a few years back. Some of it was pretty cool. Others were, in my opinion, outlandish and downright silly. The funny thing was the one display I thought that had potential to be commercially viable was criticised for not being enough like fine art. What are they teaching people nowadays? To fail in the real world? Who cares about what you think is art, it's about what people value. And if value in the art world is defined by peer-reviewed naval gazing, then we're in trouble. However, I'm not saying there isn't a place for fine art and that it all has to be about money. Sorry for the mini rant.

Before you study ballet or you decide to become an astrophysicist or whatever, make sure it's what you are meant to do. Is this something you are passionate about, or is this something that will add value to the marketplace? What about while you are studying? Do you give up all your time, energy and money for a little pat on the back? No, you wouldn't. You do it for a piece of paper and a pat on the back. Don't just sit back and scrape through. See the end goal and be passionate about what you are doing.

If you're going for a job, you need to do all the same things that others are doing just to get in the door. Sell yourself the same as what others are doing, then add your unique selling point (USP). Don't think USP first. Think what do I need to do to meet all the requirements for the position so I can get the interview. Then add your USP about how you can add value to the business. This is the most important thing for the employer. How are you going to add to the bottom line? Are you a team player? Are you consistent? Do you take initiative and instruction? Put that front and center in your application and then emphasize that at your interview.

When you get a job what are you going to do? Just enough to make sure you get paid each week? No, you should be grateful for the opportunity to add value to that business. You should think, what is the best for my employer and how can I serve and increase value in their business? This won't go unnoticed. Usually it has a positive effect and you'll get paid according to the value you provide. You don't have to passionately love it, but do it well, because it's all part of your journey to success. You'll learn so much about adding value, consistency, loyalty, and hard work. Then when the time comes, your employer will be sad you left and give you an awesome reference for your future.

I worked in an area where people tell others that the money is in the list (your customer database). Well, that's partly true. It's more accurate to say the money is in the relationship you have with the people on the list. You can add value to your audience by enriching or entertaining them, then they will listen to your suggestions. But if you spam them and sound like every other Joe out there, you'll lose most of the people on the list pretty quickly.

How can CEOs of multinational companies command tens of millions of dollars per year? Are they worth it? Well, they are because they can increase profits for the shareholders. The money that they earn in profits is well worth the millions invested in a CEO.

You need not force the issue to let people see you're valuable. Just be yourself. Do what you know you should do. Don't seek the glory because it'll be evident to others that's what you're doing. I am not saying know your place and don't seek to go higher, but at the same time be content with where you are.

People are quick to give advice, but usually have no authority to back it up. Talk is cheap. The world is full of people who have the best intentions but miss opportunities all the time. They're not willing to take risks and step out of their comfort zone. Don't seek out advice from anyone who's not in the position you want to be in. While it's good to get good advice, do your homework and then take action with calculated risks.

Calculated Risks

To achieve financial freedom quickly you have to take calculated risks to get ahead. If you don't take the risks you can still become wealthy, but it takes so much longer. You might just be saving for standard retirement and not have much time left to put that wealth to good use. Boring, right? I mean it's good to think about the future. The problem is that it's not making the best use of your money now. If you're building passive investments, you won't have to worry about your retirement. You'll have more than enough to cover it.

We took some calculated risk in our lives:

1. Furniture

I mentioned before that I was wandering around a trade fair in the Chinese city of Guangzhou. I wasn't looking for anything in particular. But I thought if there was anything worth importing it had to be here. It was a huge place, and I looked at many things. I wandered through the furniture section pretty quickly because I knew nothing about furniture. But then, out of the corner of my eye, I saw this living room suite. It was small, but modern looking. It was in a configuration where you could pack it right down to fit in a box. You could fit 43 sets into a container (whereas most sets would be around 23). This interested me because it was maximizing the space in the container, so each suite would cost significantly less in shipping overheads. I looked at the market online and calculated the costs. Well we decided that the worst that could happen was we would break even, so we went for it. It was about USD$20,000. It was a significant outlay for us at the time.

We put all the furniture in my parent's garages. They were very accommodating to us. It sold well, and we made a good return from that initial seed outlay. We went on to lease a warehouse and a showroom for our business, so it was a reasonable success. You have to be able to see the final outcome, calculate the risks, and if it stacks up, go for it. Don't sit on these ideas for too long. Do your homework. Don't assume because others are doing it, it must be easy and you should do it too. Which brings me to the next thing we took risks with:

2. Properties
Our first property purchase had been successful for us. We'd been looking for properties for quite a while, although we didn't know what we would do with it. It ended up being a fantastic buy. I put it down more to being at the right place at the right time. Because of this experience, the next purchases we made were well-informed investment decisions. I know so many people that don't think long-term and don't know what they want to achieve with property. It's a huge investment and the decision to purchase shouldn't be an emotional one. What others do or think shouldn't be a factor. If the property ticks all the boxes, and it's on the right side of the property market, it can make you a lot of money.

I hope you got that I am not saying "just take risks." That's somewhat foolish, though not as foolish as someone who refuses to take any risks at all. Are those people really living? Take risks where you have calculated the potential pitfalls and profits. You need to be able to see that. How much is it going to cost? What is my potential profit? What could happen? What is the worst-case scenario? Who are my competitors? Who are my market demographics? You should know those things.

I had someone tell me they only needed a few hundred thousand dollars for an idea of theirs - a sure thing. Even if it was a sure thing, why take the risk with all that money, especially if it's money you need to borrow? If money is an issue, you can start some businesses with a computer, an idea and a smile. The risk is so small yet the potential profit is good. Why not start something like that?

Don't be afraid. Fear will keep you in your seat, cause you to live within your comfort zone and make you boring. Faith will grow you and your dreams, and cause you to believe in yourself to achieve all you're meant to do. You're never going to achieve anything with that fear around your neck. You need to step out in faith and take those calculated risks in order for you to be successful.

Failures are Speed Bumps on the Road to Success

A reason I have succeeded isn't that I've a better education, am smarter, had better opportunities or was at the right place at the right time. No, if you look back at the successes you'll see they've been littered with failures. I can't tell you how many, and at times it feels shameful to talk about failures. Yet, without those things, I wouldn't be where I am today. It's good to remember them whenever you feel down or find it difficult to break through. You can reflect on those times when you were failing and realize that you were only a few steps away from success. But you had to push through the pain you were experiencing in order to gain that success.

Don't be afraid to fail. You can be sure that failures will come as part of the journey. If you haven't failed at something, then you probably haven't tried hard enough. Embrace the failures and learn from them because they bring you a step closer to where you need to be. Everyone fails, it happens to the best of us. Pick yourself up, dust yourself off and get back in there.

It was said of Thomas Edison that he failed 1,000 times before he invented the lightbulb. But that wasn't his interpretation. He saw it as a part of the process. There's an old saying that you should "fail forward." As long as you are moving forward toward your goal, you'll get there. Failures are just the speed bumps on the road to success. They can slow you down, but sometimes they're necessary to go over to get to your destination. If you turn around and go in the wrong direction you will obviously never reach your destination or goal.

Enjoy the Journey

Know that the journey no matter how tough is all part of the process of helping you to become who you're meant to be. In fact, the harder or more difficult the experience or journey, the more beneficial it can be to you. For then you can see who you really are and how much you can handle. It can help to get rid of things that'll hinder you in the future and to strengthen your skills in the present.

You should realize that the position you're in right now is part of the journey. Don't despise your job, your university course, or whatever it is. But embrace what you do with vigor because you're being added to and as you grow you add value. Sometimes you'll be "stuck" in a season where you don't seem to be going anywhere or are struggling with difficult situations. Don't despair during these times. How you deal with the situations and your attitude to them now will determine your success later. You are also being stretched and becoming stronger in your skillset to deal with issues in the future.

What Should You Produce?

It can be hard to come up with an idea of a product to sell or a service you will provide as a producer. Some would argue that you should go where the market is, where people are spending money, and not to let your passions or your hobbies guide you because it won't necessarily lead to the money. I would argue that your primary motivation shouldn't be about money. Remember that letting greed dictate leads down a slippery slope. You should always be in control of your desires.

At times, doing something that isn't aligned with vision helps drive you towards it. For example, I realized I didn't want to work in or be in a certain place, so I did all that I could to get out of there. Negative experiences are powerful motivators to push you to pursue what you want.

It's best to focus on your vision, but there's a qualifier for that. It has to be sustainable. That is, you actually have to be able to earn money to survive. Your passion might be tap dancing, but there's generally not much money to be made in many types of dancing. But you can find ways and means to be involved in the area, like teaching dance or something along those lines.

People assume that low-paying wages aren't going to get you anywhere. Generally, that is true. But my wife and I were on low wages. In fact, there were many years where we weren't earning any wages at all. The point is that whatever you're doing and earning, you can be creative with what you have. And in some ways, a job that is part-time gives you time to figure out more ways to manage your wealth.

In certain cultures, we've seen people set up identical product offerings side by side. The success of this strategy comes down to the position of your shop and the relationships you've formed. This isn't what we'd call having a competitive advantage where you stand out from the crowd. So, you should do market research to see what is selling or what people are buying and how you can compete. You shouldn't do it the other way round, by finding a product then trying to match it to the market.

Also, people think, "If my product is unique, then people will love it and they will buy." That is a load of baloney. It's not true and has never been true. It can be very costly trying to be the exception. The tried and true is this: Sell what is already selling.

Sell What is Already Selling

Now, you should know that when you start a business you should sell what is already selling. Don't think that you'll do something completely different and it'll make lots of money. It hardly ever happens. People buy what they understand. If you have to explain it to them, then they're not already in the market for what you have. You can be a little better than your competitors by having higher quality or a lower price (not recommended). Or you could emphasize something that your competitors don't have, or even something they might have but they don't advertise (sneaky).

You are not your customer and although you may want what you offer, others may not. Entrepreneurs differ from consumers and don't share the same purchasing habits as them. Try selling in the market and see if people buy. If they do, then you might have a business idea that's worth pursuing. If they don't buy, then you can move on to something else.

Look to help people fill a need or solve a problem. For example with furniture, people are either looking for something cheap to fill a functional need, or designer to meet an aesthetic need. You can't be high-end and budget at the same time. You have to choose. So, you need to understand your market, but also the type of product that people like. Now you might like bamboo furniture, but if that style was on trend 20 years ago, you might not get any customers. Or you might be five years ahead of your time, so no one desires what you are selling yet. You need to sell what people want, and you can know that by observing what is already selling.

But if others are selling the same kind of furniture, then why will people choose yours? That's where you decide on your unique selling point (USP). It could be based on price or warranty or features. Sometimes there can be a glut in the market, then you'll need to adapt. I have experienced this. But like I said, if you have a USP, then you'll still get a disproportionate market share. Because your USP shines a spotlight on your differences where the rest of the market is the same.

Being in the Zone

Being in the zone means you understand your market and are actively looking for opportunities. It'll help you to see things that others don't and to be quick to jump on opportunities as they arrive. For our software business, I often monitored sites with new software scripts. Every now and then I would see something I thought would make a great bit of software. For example, I saw a script which sped up website page loading so you wouldn't recognize that it was loading. I asked my coder to take a look, and within 30 minutes he made a simple website software based on this script. (It was open source, so it could be used for commercial projects). So, within half an hour I had a product I could sell.

Now, if you're just entering a market you wouldn't have seen this. You need to study the market to understand what it wants and know if people will pay you for it. This only happened because of consistency. It's like educating yourself by learning a language. You don't learn it all in one sitting. You learn it one class at a time, over a period of years, then master it so you can reference it at any time.

In real estate, you should research over many months about the market. Then you can see what's selling and what kind of property gives the best returns. When something comes along that's a bargain within your parameters, you can move to buy it in quick time. If you're new to the market you don't have all that loose data floating around in your head. You shouldn't make any decisions lightly. They say that the "deal of the century" comes around every month or so. You just need to keep in the game and focused. Another example was when we were renovating, we were able to spot a few bargains. We bought more than we needed, sold the excess for profit, so it reduced the cost of the items we kept for ourselves.

Passive Income

As mentioned, one of the finance liberation principles is to earn passive income. What is passive income? It's where you receive an ongoing income based on a service provided. If you can produce a passive income, then you might find financial freedom quicker. Someone who charges an hourly rate is still subject to actually doing the work. Imagine a lawyer who receives $250 per hour. If something happens to them so they can't work, then they don't get paid.

Examples of passive income include:
- Rental properties
- Website hosting
- Software as a service
- Subscription services, like pay TV or phone line rental

One area where I received a recurring passive income was being an affiliate. An affiliate is someone who promotes another product and a third party buys that product. The commission is paid to the affiliate. This is one area where you can find commissions that give recurring passive income. I promoted some software products in the past that had a recurring payment attached to it. I did the work once in promoting the product. But I got paid monthly because people kept their subscriptions with the service. There's a certain percentage of subscribers who will drop off within the first few months. Eventually, you'll only have the fans or those who have forgotten they have the subscription. Yes, it does happen (even I have done this!). So you would either need to send more traffic to the offer or to other offers to be able to keep up a certain income. Unfortunately for me, the software producers discontinued their service. That means I don't receive any more commissions.

The easiest way to convince people to buy a recurring product is to first have them buy one of your products. Because they've purchased from you and are happy with the product, they tend to trust you. A happy customer is willing to listen to a recommendation for something that might help them. Of course, this might take time and money, but it doesn't have to be expensive. I built software apps. They typically cost anywhere from $200-$4,000, and I expected a multiplication of that cost in profit when I sold them.

Let's summarize: A producer is someone who has vision, passion and adds value to the marketplace. You need a vision, otherwise, you'll lose focus and not achieve anything in particular. You should have a passion for what you do, otherwise you will lose interest when the going gets hard, and I assure you, it will get hard. You need to add value. Provide something that your target audience wants and are willing to pay you for. Remember, you're not your audience. Get these elements right and you'll be a producer and well on your journey to finance liberation.

7/ Step Four: Become a Marketer

It's a given that you should produce a good product, but you'll also need to advertise that product, and the message that sells it is called marketing. Marketing is presenting an offer and trying to convince others to take up what you're offering. Marketing is more important than the product you're selling. You might have the best product in the world, but if no one knows about it or understands why they need it, then they won't buy it. They need to have a compelling reason to take up the offer. Everyone is involved in marketing, even if you aren't a business person. For example, if you apply for a job you'll present yourself in the best possible light to make a good impression.

Know Your Market

Don't just assume that you know your market. You're not your customer, and you don't purchase the same things they do. As someone who sells, you are very different from those that are consumers of products. You should see through the eyes of your potential customers. For my software business in the marketplace where I sold, the majority of buyers were small business owners over the age of 40. I needed to know the demographics of my potential clients, so I could give them what they wanted.

Our furniture business started in a couple of my father's garages. How can you sell furniture from a garage? Well, through the medium of the internet, you can now do things that couldn't have been imagined a few years ago. It opened up a whole new way of doing business. We were selling furniture on a site called TradeMe (like ebay) in NZ. People could see pictures, but couldn't try out the furniture. They had to take it on faith that what they were seeing was good quality and not just photoshopped pictures. The first container sold well, and we had to order another container so we would have enough stock. It's competitive now, but when we started, there wasn't much competition.

Understanding and taking advantage of a shift in buying behaviors is a great way to get ahead. You can position yourself as a professional but still operate out of a garage. I am not saying you should lie, but if you market well, the perception others have of you can make you look better than you are in reality.

Speak their Language

We were in China running an English Training School. We didn't know the market and couldn't speak the language. It's crazy to think about it now, but it was a fantastic experience and we learned so much. How did we do? We did okay, it wasn't a total failure. The previous owners of the business poured money into it for negative returns. It was seriously hemorrhaging money. We obviously didn't want to continue losing money, so we cut expenses to try to keep it afloat. We had a manager who helped with our ideas and translate them for the Chinese market. It worked okay, but we were just starting out so we had little marketing experience.

No matter which market you are in you have to speak your customer's language. That might seem obvious as we couldn't have English advertising in a Chinese market, but understanding another culture takes time. You have to speak in a way that means something to your customer. If you're saying something that means nothing to them, then they'll not listen. For example, if my target market is business people, then I shouldn't speak to them the same way I would to teenagers who want to learn general English. It's a totally different language and approach.

The Product Comes a Distant Second Place

Your product is not the most important thing. Marketing is more important. If your message is not listened to, then it's doomed to failure. You'll see this in many diverse markets where something that is not great sells well, but the best product that's ahead of its time fails dismally because of bad marketing.

I will use the company Apple as an example again. I know, you think I am a hater. I use them to illustrate a point about product popularity. Because they're so huge everybody has heard of them which makes them an excellent example. Many people would suggest that Apple is a fantastic innovator, which could be true in some ways. But all their major products are based on other products that were already available.

First-mover advantage gives a company the edge if consumers see them as the market leader. But if the company produces something that people don't understand, they won't buy it. But what if it's the best product in the world and everyone needs one? It doesn't matter; it's not important. They don't understand it, so they won't buy it. For example, the iPod was basically a glorified MP3 player. The MP3 player had been around for years before the iPod came out. I remember someone showing me one and I thought it looked cool. But my first thought was, "What about all of my CDs"? "What would I do with them"? I didn't really understand the concept. So, the MP3 player was already in the market, then Apple released something very similar. But the world was ready because now they understood the concept.

The iPhone was certainly not the first smartphone either. Not by a long shot. There were others who had been dominant in this market, which was aimed at business people. Then Apple targeted the general population and they took to it. Some may argue that they were the first to do it "right" or "their way." But that's beside the point. That's an argument about design features, not product development or innovation.

Lastly, we can look at the iPad. This again was not a new concept. In fact, around ten years before the iPad, Microsoft released a similar product, which failed miserably. It didn't take off at all. Brilliant concept, but wrong timing to the market. Now, it could also be argued that it wasn't a great product, or that Microsoft was aiming at the wrong market, but the fact was that in all these cases Apple was many years behind in innovation and they weren't new ideas. Even now, if you look at some of the specifications for an Apple product compared to a rival, you see much higher specs with the rival.

How is it that Apple can get away with this? It's because Apple has shown itself to be a great marketing company. Their product is good enough. I don't want to cause offense unnecessarily to Apple fanboys. The product is okay. But their marketing is fantastic. You don't need to be the first, you just need to understand the market and get in at the right time.

The Reasons People Buy

Marketing is an art and a science, meaning that you can be creative in how you present your offer. But there are certain factors that should be present to get the desired conversions.

Understanding
People have to understand what you're trying to sell them. If they don't understand, they won't buy.

Trust
People have to trust that what you're saying is true.

Fear of Loss
People need to fear that if they don't purchase then they'll lose out on something that might help them.

Part of an Exclusive Club
If you can make people feel that by purchasing they'll have something special, then they'll want to be part of it. If you had a certain group of famous people using a product, then others will have the desire to get that product. It makes them feel that they can be like those people.

Scarcity or Sense of Urgency
If you have a limited quantity of products or it's available

only for a limited time, then people will be eager to get it. Because they fear they may not be able to get it in the future.

I used to sell software in a marketplace called the Warrior Forum. I would produce and sell software that I knew the market wanted and understood. I knew this by researching what was selling and the comments others had left on the forum. I started the pricing at around $7 and increased the price by 5 cents every few sales. This was automated. People always want to get something for the best price, so it created a sense of urgency for those interested in buying. At the beginning, people said they would wait for reviews. When good reviews appeared it helped with sales as people began to trust that the product was useful. When someone influential promoted the product a lot of people bought because they wanted to be part of the action.

Don't Over Hype but *Do* Over Deliver

People are expecting to get what they pay for. They rarely expect to get more than what they pay for. If they do get more, then they're usually pleasantly surprised. This is good because it means that refund rates will be lower. And if people are happy, they might talk about it, giving you word-of-mouth advertising. This is golden. How can you over deliver? By adding an extra bonus or a promise of something free next time they purchase from you. This can be anything that will help the customer think they've scored a good deal. Hopefully, it will make them happy to do business with you again.

In selling software online I tended to do things a little different than most. I was extremely honest about my products. Strange, I know. That doesn't work for everyone as some people are turned off. But in a world where everyone seems to be over-hyping and under delivering on their promises, it helps people to trust what you have to say. I didn't do it as a marketing ploy as such. It was more me being my playful self and having some fun. That was my personal operating style and opinion.

Get Them Into the Funnel

You want to get the word out to as many people as you can. People who have purchased from you will likely not view your message as spam because they know and can trust you (we hope). If you can get people into your sales funnel, then you can present your message to them. But if they've not purchased from you, there are ways to get them to become part of your audience.

Examples of ways to get people into the funnel
- Sign up forms on a website
- Podcasts
- Getting them to join a group on Facebook, Twitter or LinkedIn
- Selling them something that has a large value at cost or a loss leader. You can present your offer to them in a way that benefits you both
- Giving something away for free. The cheapest way to do this would be to give away an information product (e.g. a free ebook) so that the potential customer signs up to get that information

An example of this is a software product funnel. If I could get people to buy my software, then I would present them with another offer. I would have a front end offer, which was the first product. Then I would present them with an upsell, which would have extra features or be a product that complemented the other one. It didn't have to end there. Depending on their actions, they would be presented with other offers.

Repeat Customers

It's cheaper to sell to the same customers than to get new customers. You should always be on the look-out to acquire new customers, but it usually comes at a high price. You might have to run some sort of advertising campaign to get new customers to see your product. In contrast, with existing customers, you already know that they're buyers. If there's a possibility they might buy from you again, you should position something in front of them to give them that opportunity. This can be free advertising because you already have all their details (at least you should).

When someone bought one of my software products they went onto my subscriber list. When I produced a new product or was an affiliate for another product, I would email those on this list. Most times, I would give away quite a bit in commissions to affiliates to promote my products. I did this in the hope to gain subscribers to my list. That way, the next time I promoted to the customers on the list I wouldn't have to pay the commissions to affiliates. I would keep the entire amount of the sale.

People's Perception of You is Greater than Reality

It doesn't matter what the reality is. If people think of you in a certain way, then you are that to them. They might think you are a fly-by-night scam artist, when in fact you have operated your business for years with integrity. They might think that you're a wealthy, high-flying executive, but the truth might be that you borrowed your suit, live in your parent's basement and don't even have a bank account. The reality of your situation is not seen by others (unless you show them), but their perception of you is what is true to them. It's like the statement, "first impressions last." You need to present yourself to potential customers in such a way so their first impression is the best one.

Look at the example of our furniture business when we first started out. People may have assumed that we had an expensive showroom decked out with our latest models. But in reality, we had the furniture stacked up in my father's garages with only two models to choose from. If they assumed we were a top class designer company, then they might be eager to buy, but if they knew that we sold out of a garage, they might not want to take the risk. Do I need to tell them that I am operating out of a garage? Does it change the quality of the product? No. It's a perception of what you're getting. You're more likely to assume the quality is better if you buy out of a showroom than out of someone's garage. So, without lying to people, we want them to see us in the best possible light. If they asked us, we could tell them that we're selling to them out of a garage. But why would that be important for us to tell them? If we told them it was a certain color, and it was a different color, then that would be lying. We don't need to share details that the potential customer doesn't need to know.

Fake it Till You Make it?

This is an often-repeated phrase similar to what I was describing above. However, in general what people mean by it is that even if you don't know something, fake it like you do know it. This is bad advice because you are essentially lying to gain an advantage. With my furniture example, I could have lied and said my designs were made by some certain designer. If someone asks you to do some work you have no experience in, but you act like you have experience in it, that's a lie. These seem pretty obvious, but the lines can easily get blurred when you are trying to make it. Which brings me to my next point . . .

Position Yourself as an Authority

People say you should do this to attract clients to not only work with you but also to pay you premium prices. The problem is that if you're not the authority and don't have all the experience and connections you claim, you're being deceitful.

In the above examples, you could actually do some of these and become successful. There's a temptation to fast-track success by lying to make it seem like you have it all together. I know of a marketer that claimed he had all these connections with some famous marketers. He also proclaimed himself as the best in the world at what he did. Well, he is doing well financially. It seemed to pay off big time for him. Notice how I said, seemed. You see, the thing is that if you compromise in one area, you'll be tempted to compromise again and again. It'll be difficult to resist because you've already crossed that line.

If you are in fact an authority (or at least have done what you said), then you can legitimately claim authority in your area of expertise. People want to take advice from those who are experts, rather than some poser who only wants to take their money. It may mean that you might have to give more of your time initially to show that you know what you are talking about. You can then position yourself above the competition.

Sales Formula

There's a basic formula for making sales. You need some ingredients. First, you need something to sell, a product or service. Second, you need to have a marketing message. You need to convince the potential customer that they should buy from you. Finally, you need to get traffic to view your message. You should have a quality product, otherwise, you'll get refunds and no repeat customers. Also, traffic should be targeted to your offer. If the traffic is general and has no interest in your offer, then conversions will be very low and the price per lead will be high. The most important element is the marketing message.

Product + Traffic + Message = Conversions

This works in any market. See examples below:

Example A: Physical Product

If you own a coffee shop, the equation would look something like this:

Coffee + People walking by + Incentive of a free muffin with coffee purchase = Increase in sales

Example B: Digital Product:

Software + Facebook ads + New software that solves your business problems = More clicks

Example C: Service:

If you own or operate a service, such as accountancy, the equation would look something like this:

Accounting + Yellow Pages + The five rules of accounting revealed = More calls

Marketing is the most essential ingredient in selling. But it shouldn't be overemphasized at the expense of the other elements covered in this book. Some of the concepts of marketing can be a bit manipulative, yet you can still be a good marketer and keep your morals, you just need to be creative. This wasn't designed to be an exhaustive list of everything about marketing. But even with this lesson, if you see it as a part of the whole package of this model, you'll do well. Maybe even better than some so-called marketing experts.

8/ Step Five: Become an Investor

You have to put all your millions somewhere, and under your mattress isn't generally a great idea. You should invest your money to make it grow. In this chapter, we look at the finance liberation investment principles and the different investment types.

I'm not a full-time obsessed expert investor. This chapter isn't designed to be a detailed guide on every aspect of investing. What I do share with you are the finance liberation principles that'll help you to filter out bad investments. It'll guide you into making wise decisions rather than giving dated investment advice.

Investment Principles

1. Understand the Investment

People are generally lazy. We like to take the easy path. I see plenty of people invest without doing much homework at all. They may go to a property seminar, watch a couple of videos about the stock market and then believe they can make an informed investment decision. It takes time to understand investments. You should understand the risks involved and the potential returns. You should also understand the time that your money will be tied up. All these things need to be considered and evaluated before investing. Don't rush, otherwise, you are basically gambling, not investing. If you intend to invest in something without understanding the risk and reward, you can expect to lose big in your gamble.

Maybe you'll miss out on a few opportunities, but they come along quite often and you'll be able to spot a good one the next time it comes. The pain of missing out on an opportunity helps you to see what you missed and be aware the next time it arises. If you thought something was an opportunity and later see it would've been a bad investment, you gain wisdom. Your experience on how much things cost and how businesses operate is valuable. Sure you could learn these things in a classroom setting. But there's nothing quite like real life experience in how things work.

I was reminiscing with a friend the other day about how we should've brought many houses in a particular time in the market, as we would be much wealthier than we are now. Things are clearer with hindsight. That was our first taste of the property market. We hadn't gone through any cycles of boom or bust before and we couldn't have predicted the exponential growth in prices. It was an opportunity that was lost and never to be regained, yet it was a valuable lesson about how things work. We can see opportunities now we didn't understand before and we can make informed decisions.

You Can't Trust Most People

This seems like a terrible thing to say, not to trust people. But here is the thing, you're responsible for your own life. That might sound pretty simple, but it's quite profound. You can't blame others for any predicament you get into after following someone's advice. Do your due diligence and find out if what they're telling you is true.

You have to be careful whose advice you follow. Especially in things like property and shares which have cycles. I wouldn't follow their advice if they hadn't gone through a few of the cycles over say a 20-year period. They haven't had the full experience of the market cycles. Not that they can't learn this from others and trends, but I see many dangerous teachings out there.

Whom do you want to emulate? Those who seem to have it all together, but their finances are like a pack of cards and could fall over any moment? Or those who seem like an average Joe or Joe-ess, but they've built their lives upon unchanging rock solid principles? The rain falls on each of them, but who will remain standing after the storm passes over?

This might be somewhat offensive, but from what I have experienced, I wouldn't trust a real estate agent as far as I could throw one. Not that they don't know what they're talking about, but they have an agenda, to part you with your money. Any advice on how good a property is and the potential earnings should be fact checked.

We had a real estate agent sell a house for us a couple of years ago. They referred to themselves as professional, but the service provided was anything but professional. They quoted a figure and we signed a contract. A few weeks later after doing so-called market research, the new sales figure was 10-20% less than the quote. They proceeded to tell us the house was in such a bad state that it was unrentable (even though it was in the same state as when they first saw it). They were trying to paint us into a corner to sell and get our expectations down.

The auction day was even worse. They gave advice to put the absolute lowest reserve price we could go for at the auction. We figured out that if there were only a couple of bidders and one pulled out early it would sell at a low price. That's exactly what happened. Had we followed their advice, we would've sold for around $50K less than what we got. It didn't meet reserve at auction and the property was passed in. The agent negotiated and got a price we weren't happy with. They pleaded with us to be reasonable. We said no and gave a figure we could sell at. The agent was so negative and wouldn't take our offer to the purchaser. But because we pushed we got the price $30K higher. We settled on a figure we thought was good, but not fantastic.

During the negotiation, we wanted to sell the furniture that was there with the house. We clarified with the agent that we were basically going to hand over the keys to our house and walk away. Later we found out that the agent said we would clear out the garage (because an internal access garage is not considered part of the house?). This could've been costly for us to either clear it out or to battle with the lawyers. We told the agent that agreement they had made with the purchaser was their agreement and not ours. There were some other late issues as well which the agent should've made us aware of. All this happened while we were living overseas in Fiji!

Don't take people at face value when you're dealing with money. When people have an agenda, especially around money, you can bet things get warped. Don't trust people to give you good advice, unless they have proven themselves over and over again.

For any investment, you'll need to get off your butt, do the research and find out how it works for yourself. Most people can be pretty lax when it comes to due diligence. They spend lots of money yet don't find out exactly what the facts are. Do your homework and you'll find that you will start to make wise decisions. It could take awhile before you take the plunge into something scary, but make sure you have all the information you need to make an informed decision.

Don't Follow the Crowd

The crowd in most cases is generally wrong. Why is that? Maybe because they just have enough information to be dangerous. As the saying goes, "A little bit of knowledge is a dangerous thing." Perhaps they see things from one angle and assume it's correct without considering they might need to view it from a different angle. When Joseph Kennedy (JFK's father) heard the shoeshine boy talk about the stock market, he knew it was time to get out. He sold a considerable amount just before the stock market crashed. In real estate there's a saying, "When others are selling, I'm buying and when others are buying, I'm selling."

So what if everyone seems to be buying property or shares

or gold. Warning bells should go off in your head seeing that happen. You should know that it's just a matter of time before it all crashes around everyone's ears. People will ask, "what happened?" They didn't see it coming and start blaming others, but the simple fact of the matter is they were driven by greed. Trying to push too hard on something to get money is greed and it'll always come back to bite you. Notice I said always. Yes, always. Why do I say this? I mean surely there are cases where greedy people have made a ton of money, but they're not wiped out in a big crash? Yes, I am sure that's true. But if they have compromised because of greed and not dealt with the issue, you can bet they'll do it again. One day, when they're greedy, they'll get bitten. It's only a matter of time.

People are like lemmings and will follow what others are doing even if they're going head first over a cliff. They may have studied and be well informed, yet intelligence is not the same as wisdom. What do I mean? You can be very educated in a particular area, let's say it's in business and you can ace your exams. You can get to the top of your class and wow your friends with all sorts of fancy sounding words and witty comebacks. But life is not always clear cut. The real world is not like a laboratory where everything can be controlled. You have to make decisions that can carry considerable risk. You also need the wisdom to know when to walk away or pursue the opportunity. That requires you to figure it out yourself. You should understand what you want to invest in and not trust the know-it-all slick talking salesman.

Sometimes the crowd will even become angry if you don't tow the line. For example, let's talk about something not money related, but gay marriage. I know, a bit off topic and all. There was a debate recently about gay marriage. Views have changed about this quite significantly in one generation and there is a lot of name-calling on both sides. Why is this? Aren't we allowed freedom of speech? Why should a difference of opinion cause someone to think that they hate you or want to cause you harm? Why is it assumed that someone's position is that of an ignorant bigot before hearing why they believe as they do? I won't say any side is right or wrong. I am only using this example so you can see the emotion involved and sides that are taken. It's not to prove any kind of point about the topic at all, so don't take it the wrong way. This is hard to do with topics involving money and it's more subtle. Yet it's still there and you should see that popular opinion is not always, and in fact hardly ever, right. So, don't be dictated to by others about what you should think or feel. Don't back down on what you believe because others will call you out. I'm not saying be different on purpose, but be prepared to be challenged on what you believe by common dissenters who might think you're crazy.

The crowd is trying to drag you into their way of thinking, trying to get you to agree with them because it's popular. But generally, the crowd is wrong. I am not saying that everyone you talk to is the crowd and you should think of yourself as superior, not at all. You'll recognize the language of the crowd as saying things like the market only goes in one direction. Or real estate agents are saying it's the right time to buy. Or look at gold it has doubled, I am sure it will do it again.

Given that successful people only make up a minority of the population, you have to wonder about the difference between them and others. Yes, they have the right mindset and had the opportunity and all that, but they also work hard and had focus. Most people aren't willing to do this or only willing to do the bare minimum to get by. So in taking risks with their money, they fail to research, and follow what other followers are doing. It's like the blind leading the blind. They think they know the truth, but in fact, they're following the rest of the crowd who are heading off the cliff.

2. Avoid a Get Rich Quick Mentality

There are basically two ways to become financially liberated. The slow way or the fast way. I know you're pretty disappointed, right? You thought it would be some deep and meaningful truth? Sorry to disappoint you. But wait, let me explain.

The slow way is a methodical process of being careful with your finances and planning the future. The fast way is coming up with some way to bypass the above process and generally compromise freedoms or choices. Okay, so I have spun the above definitions to make a point about which one I think is best, which is of course (pause for effect), the slow way. Sometimes slower is better. In our fast paced world, we want instant gratification.

When I say slow, I don't mean snail's pace, or it'll take forever, but there's a process to learn and it usually takes time. Our journey to financial freedom took around 10 years, on and off. It could've been much quicker if we were better informed or didn't travel as much. If I said that you could start with little but have financial freedom in around 10 years, would you say that was slow?

Slow is probably the wrong word here as it's not exactly motivational. I can quite happily look back now and say that the time taken to gain financial freedom was slow. Although I didn't think it was slow at the time, only that I had to do whatever was needed to reach the goal. But as most people retire in their late 60s (and still need superannuation), retiring

25 years earlier must seem express pace. It would probably be more accurate to say there's a need to learn the systems to produce wealth. Boring, I know. I'll keep with the word slow as it's easier to remember.

Get Rich Quick?

Please don't think that I am against getting rich quick. There's nothing morally wrong with it, but you've probably not seen all the hard work that has gone on behind the scenes. The thing generally with those who are trying to get rich quick is they don't want to do the work required to get rich.

Take the time to learn the process of how money flows. Money will flow in a certain direction or directions. Usually, it's away from us. Anyone who has not had experience in dealing with money the right way will find that money flows away from them. However if we understand how money works we can change the direction so that our net worth increases over time rather than decreases. This, I believe, can only happen for us through time and experience. Those who come into wealth quickly haven't had this experience with money. It's very easy for the money to magically disappear from them and they don't know where it has gone.

We hear of those cases of people who got rich quick, with that great idea that "took off", winning the lottery or gaining a huge inheritance. Don't plan and dream about it because you'll end up disappointed. Poor you...literally. A large proportion of those people who win the lottery lose everything within a short time. If they haven't been prudent with their finances before the big win, they'll most likely be in a worse position after. Effective money management is a life skill that many don't learn. If they're thrown into a situation where they have more than they can manage, then things can go downhill fast. There are lessons you learn along the way to becoming wealthy that are better to learn before you get there.

Shortcuts are for Dummies

People are always looking for a shortcut to wealth without pain or hard work. It's human nature to want to avoid pain and take the easy path. There's nothing inherently wrong with that. You have to learn some things before you go out there and make your money. Well, actually, that's not true, you don't need to learn things. It just helps if you want to keep the money and not have it slip through your fingers. Don't think that you can spend on anything you want and it not affect you like it does others. You're only fooling yourself. I'm not saying it's impossible to find shortcuts. In fact, with the internet it's more likely in our time than any other time in history. You only need to follow some simple rules if you want to have that money not mysteriously vanish.

3. Eliminate Debt Risk

Debt in a lot of circles is seen as good. It will get you what you want faster, but most debt actually enslaves you. You can't get ahead financially if you're in debt.

Car Loan Debt

If you bought a new car for $30,000 with a car loan at 9% over 7 years, the cost would be $483/month. It equates to total interest of $10,544 and the total amount paid for the car excluding operating expenses is $40,532.

New cars can depreciate pretty quick. So quick in fact that the moment you drive it off the yard you might have lost up to a quarter of the value. The car might only be worth around $22,000. After the 7 years, the car you paid over $40,000 for might be worth less than $9000, over $30,000 less than what you paid. How's that for wasting money? Generally depreciating assets are bad investments.

Student Loan Debt

Suppose you took out a student or tuition loan of $50,000. It would take over 4 years (assuming no or low interest) to pay back on a $40,000 per year salary, assuming you have around $10,000 per year left after taxes and other expenses. If your course takes four years, you could be looking at a nearly a decade before you are at a zero net worth! Wowzers!

Household Debt

Okay, what about an appreciating asset like buying a house? That must be a good debt to have right? Suppose you took out a loan of $300,000 at 6% (approx historic average figure) interest over a term of 30 years (typical timeframe). The total that you would pay would be around $647,000. That is a lot of money to come up with! Obviously, it's less if you pay it off earlier or the interest rate is on average lower. People might tell you to look for areas where you will get capital gains in the future. Well, you will need huge capital gains just so that you can break even. It can happen and is likely to happen in major cities, but it's not certain and is a very long term strategy.

So, is there any kind of debt that is good? Only if it meets one of our finance liberation principles of using other people's money. I don't mean just getting a mortgage. You need someone to pay for that mortgage or debt. If someone else is paying for the debt and any other costs while leaving you with some profit, then it might be good. That's because it wouldn't be dependent on you to pay the debt. Relying on one person's income to pay for that debt puts you in a very dangerous position. If the income stops coming through you could lose whatever the debt is for.

4. Get Multiple Income Sources

Often you'll hear about the virtues of diversification. It's investing in multiple investment types to minimize risk. But most "investors" don't have a good understanding of many of the different investment types, so, they're not necessarily making good investment decisions. You can still minimize risk by instead investing in multiple income sources. What's the difference? If you understand an investment type well, why invest in some other type you don't have a good understanding of? It's like a pro golfer taking up basketball as well, in case something happens to his golf career. It doesn't make sense. They are both sports, but they have unrelated skillsets.

You can instead get multiple income sources from the investment types that you understand well. For example, right now, we're invested in property and bank term deposits. Many investment gurus wouldn't be happy with that kind of spread. But if you have many income sources from investments you understand well, then your risk is small, and you will have less stress.

If you understand the four investment principles laid out above you will be able to spot a good investment regardless of what it is. We will now give an overview of the different investment types.

Investment Types

A. Currency

Savings in a Bank

You want to put your money into a bank that gives you decent interest but also has some protection if there's an economic crash. That's insurance if things go sour in the financial markets. Some countries have a deposit guarantee scheme in place. It makes sure that if the bank fails that the investors (savers) will get their money back. Not all countries have this insurance scheme so it's good to know what level of protection your money has.

We sold a property and decided to put the money in a few banks. Our country doesn't have the deposit guarantee, so we have most of the money in a bank that's owned by the government. We thought they would have a greater protection as opposed to private banks. Many banks invest in the stock market, so they can be caught out if the stock market crashes. Also, banks don't actually hold all of your money. They can borrow against a multiplication of the money that they have on hand.

Inflation nowadays means that you aren't making your money work for you by only putting it in the bank. This isn't a good long-term option. We have a sizeable amount of money in term deposits. That's because we are happy with the low risk and the income we receive in interest. We also don't want to spend the time researching investments as we are enjoying retirement. We will look to invest the money elsewhere in the near future to get a better ROI.

Bonds

Bonds are basically a loan you lend to an institution. Generally, these are bonds that the government will issue. They're usually a safer bet than putting your money in a bank as they're controlled by the government. There will only be an issue if the government itself became bankrupt. You can get bonds that businesses issue, but you are dealing with businesses that can falter. In my limited opinion, you would get better returns if you were to invest in the companies rather than lend to them. We did not use bonds at all to help us in becoming financially free.

Currency Trading, Gold, Silver and Precious Materials

This market can fluctuate greatly, even within a short amount of time. Sometimes you have to hold the actual resource, and it can cost money to hold it. Obviously, with foreign currency, you can hold it in the bank. In times of recession, this is often seen by many to be a safe haven for their money if there ever was such a thing.

We use one currency for our term deposits, another for our day to day living, and another for international payments. Although we have savings in a few currencies, it's for convenience, not for trading to gain financial freedom.

B.   Business

Businesses produce products that the market wants. However it goes beyond producing products to sell, to building a viable business you can sell in the future. Not all things that can be sold should be or could be a business.

You should try to start your business with the least outlay possible. Some would advise consulting a lawyer and an accountant before starting a business. You will only need to consult professionals when you have shown that the market wants what you are offering. Being a producer, you should sell what sells and have a USP that sets you apart from the competition. Until people buy, you have just got an idea not a business. I have started many businesses and few of them would have benefited from accountants or lawyers advice before I started them. You should focus on what to sell, your pricing and your market demographics. Those professionals don't give you that information. You need to keep it simple at the beginning, not worry about business structure.

Entrepreneurs are likely, after a time, to become bored with their business and look for something else to start. The great thing about business is that if it becomes profitable, it's worth a multiplication of its earnings to someone willing to buy it. Hopefully you've already been getting a decent ROI before you sell. Obviously you won't be able to earn from it anymore, but that might not matter if you get a big payout.

From the beginning, set targets to keep you motivated and then decide, when you reach those target points, whether to take the business forward or cash out. These may change depending on your circumstances. For example, if there's a recession you might find that no one is looking to buy a business, even though it's profitable. So it might pay to press on to another target and push through the recession. You shouldn't allow yourself to cruise aimlessly. You never want to be in a position where you're forced to sell. If you plan your exit strategy well, you'll have something to aim for and own a valuable asset.

I had to learn this the hard way. Unfortunately, with our furniture business, we never set an exit plan. The result was that we just went through the motions with it for a few years. If we had sold during its peak we could have made a nice sum. We didn't want to run it anymore, and closed it down for a couple of years when we went to Brisbane. We were only able to sell down the stock when we had the time. In looking back, there were a couple of reasons we didn't sell it. The first reason, honestly, is that I didn't think about selling it. The second is that it would have been difficult because it was my baby. As you know, it's hard to give up things you hold dear. I would estimate we would be around $200,000 better off if we sold before closing it to move to Brisbane. Instead, we had the hassle of running something we didn't want and had to store and sell down the stock. So, it added another 2-4 years of time we could have directed elsewhere. This loss is significant when you add up the time and money we can never get back.

Shares (Mutual and Index Funds, Super Schemes etc)

Personally, I haven't had a great experience with the share-market. We did not use stocks to gain our financial freedom. So, the outline here won't satisfy proponents of the stock-market. My wife invested with a money manager into some stocks. They basically used a software program to calculate trends. It's quite risky and I would say that this is generally not a great idea. You have no way of knowing exactly why they're investing like they are. I have been told that some of these software programs are a big part of market downturns. The software sees a trend downwards and will automatically sell. It can create a market slide because many investors are set up with these software programs. Pretty scary stuff. The software also picks up on stocks you already have that are selling cheap and buys more. This happened to my wife, and she ended up with a load of worthless stocks.

If you decide you want to invest in shares, then make sure you know what you are investing in. You should know how shares work and what sort of returns to expect. You should be investing in the company, by researching the company's financial position. Don't invest into something that's being promoted as lucrative.

Many people have made great amounts of money in the sharemarket, and some are extremely wealthy. Warren Buffett is one of the wealthiest investors in the world. He said that he invests in businesses, not in shares. This is great advice as many people just look at the cold hard numbers. You should realize that you are dealing with real companies and you should see how they're performing in the real world, not only by what they're giving in the form of numbers. You should understand what the business does, what assets it has, the liabilities it owes and the potential for growth. If you know these things you will be able to tell if it's under or overvalued.

These are not the only things to consider. People can be fickle. It may be a great company that has amazing features, but something might spook investors so they sell their shares or do not invest into it. People like brands and being a part of something, even if it's not profitable. Understanding people's motives for investing can help in the long and short term. Just because everyone and his dog seem to be investing in something doesn't make it a sure bet. It can be like the blind following the blind, so you can be sure that it will fall apart at some stage. Remember to do your homework.

C. Real Estate

I am going to spend more time on real estate than the other investment types. That's because, along with business, it was one of the main reasons we could retire early. Most wealthy people either use it to gain wealth or have it in their portfolio.

There's nothing else that has brought about so much wealth but also so much financial heartache as real estate. The problem that most people have with real estate is that they get emotional about it. "Oh, this is lovely, Reginald." "I can see our furniture here, Petunia." It's that emotional response that brings about a bad financial decision. I have heard people say they see the house they live in differently than they would a rental investment. Well, whether you see something as an investment or not doesn't change what it is: an investment. Of course, it won't matter if you have wads of money and you buy something for yourself based on an emotion. The problem comes when you borrow beyond your means or don't factor in price fluctuations in the market. You can get yourself into a pickle and set back your goals of financial independence years or even decades. Having said that, real estate is my personal favorite form of investment.

Real estate is where we have a lot of our wealth invested. Why? I guess because it's tangible (you can see it and imagine it). It can get your creative juices flowing on how best to use it for an asset. As I was writing this I was involved in renovating two properties, and I did most of the work myself. You can physically see the value you are adding.

We had a property which we bought for $242,000 in 2002 and we sold it late 2015 for $881,000. That is not to say that other properties haven't had a similar increase. General trends in major cities will have the property price double every 7-10 years. This has been true in cities like Auckland, NZ. But it's not true for other centers. You have to know your areas of investment and not just assume it will increase by the same kind of values. There comes a point where it will not or cannot double again. It's much easier for prices to double from $250,000 to $500,000 than to double from $500,000-$1,000,000. This is because property prices are held back somewhat by people's wages. Banks lend based on ability to pay down the loan. There's only so much risk that the banks will take on. If wages are not increasing, then the property cycle will have a limited run. People's wage increases don't usually keep up with property price increases. Sometimes it can be better to invest in several small properties than a couple of big ones. The marketability of less expensive properties is generally higher, too.

So, if property prices have doubled in the cycle, and its increases have slowed, it might be a good time to sell, and that's what we did. We realized near max potential of capital gain. We can use that capital in other investments. We get a similar income from bank interest as we were renting the property (after expenses).

In the following graph, starting from 2002, you can see that the average house price in Brisbane was around $200,000. In 2012 it averaged around $440,000. That is roughly double the price in 10 years. That goes with our projection of doubling every 7-10 years. Melbourne goes from $300,000 to over $600,000, around the doubling mark. So far, so good with the theory.

Sydney in 2002 was at $420,000 and in 2012, $650,000. This is only around 65% growth, not 100% like the other cities. It's still big growth, but not like the doubling we would like to expect. Why is this when Sydney is known to be such a hot market for property, well ahead of the other cities? We have not taken into account the fluctuations in the graph. But this is beside the point as it's the end result that counts.

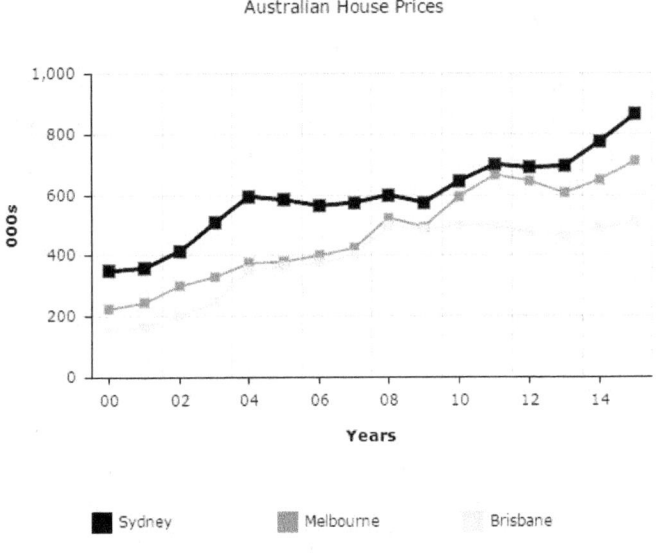

Source: RP Data, ANZ Research

Again, I believe the property market is capped by wage earnings. The banks take this into consideration when lending and won't lend over a certain level. So, I believe there's a certain range where property value cannot double. It can only rise to new highs and then recede back down to margins that are more sustainable. In 2015, Sydney's average property prices touched $1 million, a very high level. But I believe it could not go a lot higher than this unless wages rise to match the increase. Although you can follow some rules, they are not rigid or always true. A rule like property doubling every 7-10 years works in some areas with limitations.

Cycles

Property doesn't always go up in value. It also goes down. Property generally operates in a cycle, like most investments. There's sustained growth over a period of years, and then there's usually a bursting of the bubble. Property markets crash like any investment market, depending on the location and economy. There are many factors that can drive property prices up, such as immigration, the economy or wage levels. The same factors can also drive property prices down.

Leverage

You should never look at property as a nice place to live as if it were your own. In most places in the world, it's never truly yours. The government could say we want it and take it away from you. You should look at it as leverage to use for further investment. It's always difficult to get started. To get your first property usually requires money, but then you can leverage the capital increase in the first property to get others.

While we were in Brisbane, we had our properties rented out. We did not kept abreast of the changes in the market. The house prices and market rental prices had risen dramatically in Auckland. In the space of around three years, one of our properties had gone from being worth around $600,000 to closer to $1 million. This is with us doing nothing to the property. One part of it was rented for $1600p/m. Admittedly it needed a bit of work to make it look nice again. But when we had done some painting and other maintenance, we were getting around $2200p/m. So, you can see how your wealth can increase with property. We bought it a few years back for $189,000. Not only is there the capital gain on the property, but you can also get an increase in market rentals after a few years. We had changed this property from a four bedroom to a three bedroom flat and a one bedroom flat. Both flats also have an extra study or small bedroom. We were originally getting around $2000p/m for the entire house. But times have changed and we're currently getting around $3600p/m when both flats are rented.

If you are looking to buy property you should plan what you want to achieve with it. You might need to think outside the box a little bit. You could buy land, but when are you going to get a return on that investment if it's going to sit empty for a few years? And land can be very hard to sell if the market is in a downturn. If buying a property with accommodation, are you going to buy it to resell or are you going to buy and hold? A resell strategy can be a good idea, but there are many factors to take into consideration, so be sure of your profit figures.

Before purchasing a property to rent out you should calculate your return on investment. I like what many call the 1% rule. If you are to purchase a property for $200,000, then you should look to get a monthly rent of about 1% or $2000. A rule like this makes it easy to roughly calculate if something is worth considering. This can be difficult to achieve in areas where capital growth is strong. I would go for an area you would expect to increase in the coming years. However nothing is a sure thing, so invest your time in making a rock-solid plan. When the market crashes, you don't want to crash as well.

When buying property you should look for your ROI first. You need to be able to cover all the costs associated with the property and still make money. Now, you also need to take into consideration that interest rates can rise quite significantly. So, adjust your figure appropriately. Make sure you use other people's money in paying down the mortgage. Set it up so that the principal amount and interest is paid off over a period where you won't have to adjust anything. It's a nice feeling having all the income come to you directly and not to the bank.

The second most important thing is that you need to buy where people want to live. It's all about location, location location. Don't take the above as advice of buying property just anywhere. Major cities and the capital gains and market rents are different to other centers. You have to buy in the right location or very soon to be the right location. Look for property in areas where there's high demand and there's set to be growth. Outlying suburbs of major city centers would be a good example of an area for real estate investment. This is where work is readily available, and/or where there's a good university. There you will find high rental demand. There's no point buying a beautiful property where no one wants to live.

Also, check the long-term sustainability of your plan. This will help with capital gain in the future. I have a friend who brought a property as fully furnished to contractors in the area. For the first few months, he was making a fantastic ROI. But then the contractors had finished their project and rental demand dropped significantly. His potential rental return dropped by about half.

Capital Investment

A capital investment is buying something to use as a resource to make money. Let me give you an example of capital investment. A farmer will buy an expensive tractor to more efficiently do his work on the farm. Does the farmer need the tractor? No. He could do the work manually or with simpler and cheaper machinery, but he has to calculate the cost of the tractor and the time savings against income earned to see if the cost is worth it.

When we had homestays living with us, we bought some beds and heaters and sets of drawers to furnish their rooms. They effectively paid for those things. We would not have bought them otherwise. And we wouldn't have made money from having homestays if we didn't buy those items. (This is a good way to furnish your home, actually.) Most people furnish their homes with consumer items they buy for their own use. If you do that, you have used your own money after tax for those items. However if you have a homestay or boarder or use the items for business, then the profit you are getting from them can pay for the items. This way someone else is paying for the item and you will benefit from using it as well. You will save a lot more money. Do you want a new TV? Why not get a boarder in for a period of time to pay for it?

Opportunity Cost

Every choice we make in life is an opportunity cost. When you choose one option, it will mean you'll have to forgo another. For example, you might choose to go to a meeting, but that means you don't get to spend time with your family. Or purchasing this property will mean you won't be able to buy the other one you were interested in.

It's important to realize that what you gain you can reinvest. This is not only about money, but the skills you gain can be leveraged to gain more. Because you are skilled in an area you can leverage, that to add value to your company. You might be promoted to a higher position where you can add value there. You are investing whenever you spend your time, money, energy or resources. And you need to be wise in your investing.

9/ Step Six: Become a Giver

It almost seems counter-intuitive to think of giving as a means to gaining wealth. It's one of the most powerful ways to build it. Giving can exponentially increase your wealth without you needing to understand how it works. Fortunately, I explain how it works in this chapter.

Following on from the previous chapter, giving can be seen as a type of investing. Yet, giving is quite different from direct investing and so warrants its own chapter. I will explain the differences below:

Investing can be seen as making a payment into things to build monetary wealth. Giving can be seen as making a payment into people to build social wealth. Investing has an entity receiving compensation for the value they provide to a recipient. The result is the recipient doesn't feel they owe the entity because of the payment provided. Giving has a giver receiving no compensation for the value they provide to a recipient. The usual result is the recipient feels that they owe the giver because of the value received. The transaction is not complete and so the sense of obligation remains until something is given in return.

The Rule of Reciprocation

The rule of reciprocation goes something like this: Whenever you give to someone, they'll feel an obligation to give back to you. Sometimes it will be more than what was given. In some cultures, it's an unwritten rule that you must give back. In other cultures, there are no hard and fast rules, but there still is a sense of obligation to give back.

The marketing industry understands this rule and uses it to its maximum. It can be used to manipulate people into doing things they don't want to do. Of course, that which is good can be manipulated. People are unaware that they're being led to have a sense of obligation to those presenting the offer. For some, that sense of obligation others have towards them, is the reason that they give.

Someone sent me a remote controlled helicopter once as a gift. I was in an industry where people sell information and software products. One of the quickest ways to make money is to get others to promote your products (affiliates). So, even though it was a gift and he didn't ask for a promotion because I got his gift, I felt compelled to promote. Was the product any good? It was okay. But it wasn't something I would usually promote. So, in this case, the rule of reciprocation worked a treat for him.

Many times you'll receive back and you won't expect what you receive. It's a pleasant surprise. If you knew what you were going to receive back then it wouldn't be a pleasant surprise or even a gift. I had mentored a young man and helped with any questions he had. I was more than happy to spend the time as he was hungry to learn and took advice on board. I found myself in Auckland stuck renovating a property. He wanted to visit and then offered to help out. He gave his time for at least four days to help with painting and other odd jobs. I didn't expect this at all. I won't even start to calculate how much it would've cost if I hired someone. He did it out a sense of thankfulness. It was reciprocated back from what I had given him, which wasn't a burden at all and it was a genuine pleasure. Isn't this the way things should work? Not out of a desire to get ahead, but love given to others and finding its way back to us. Let your motivation be pure, and pure joy will come back to you. Giving is like sowing seed, and this sowing covers all areas of our lives.

The Law of Sowing and Reaping

The rule of reciprocation is actually subject (or a subset) to the law of sowing and reaping. In regards to giving, the rule of reciprocation is a limited model. Whereas the law of sowing and reaping is all-encompassing and covers all areas of our life, not only giving. The reciprocation model was put first to show the benefits of giving. The sowing and reaping model shows the giving and receiving criteria.

The law of sowing and reaping is this: Whatever you sow, you will reap a multiplication of that kind in the future. Imagine a farmer that's sowing wheat seed into his field. After a time, the seed sprouts, then becomes a plant which contain multiples of the original seed. So, the farmer now has much more than what he had sown. In the same way, you will always receive more than the initial sowing. If you sow an apple seed, you'll reap an apple tree with a multiple of apple seeds within each piece of fruit. You also have the potential for multiple harvests from the one tree which originated from the one seed.

Whether you like it or not, we're all subject to this law. It's like gravity. If we decide to walk off a cliff, we will fall down and get hurt. If we walk off accidentally without knowing there was a cliff, we still get hurt. It doesn't matter whether it was by accident or intentional, we're forced to exist within its rules. Gravity affects all of us all the time as does the law of sowing and reaping.

The Harvest Criteria

In order for these principles of sowing and reaping to be effective in your life, you also should be aware of the following criteria:

1. You Must Sow in the Right Season

Sowing the wrong seed (or even the right seed) in the wrong season can only be disastrous. There are times and seasons for all things. Even if all the other conditions are right, if the season is wrong, it's not going to work. There are also seasons when you shouldn't sow, like winter when the frost will destroy the seed.

People could be receptive to your idea at the right time, but if they're going on holiday, the family is sick or they lost their job, then it might not be the right season. In those situations, you might need to sow a different seed.

2. You Must Sow in Soil that is Receptive to the Seed

A farmer usually has done a lot of work before the seed can be planted. The soil must be tested to see what kind of produce it can hold. Rocks and trees must be removed. The field must be ploughed. If you sow in a soil that is not receptive to your seed, then the seed will not take or germinate. It's like the seed has been sown on hard ground.

If I knew someone was dying of thirst, I should give them something that would quench their thirst. Then the recipient would be thankful and have a sense of indebtedness to me for helping them. That should not be the purpose of giving, but the benefit if it comes to that. If I, however, decided to give this person a toothbrush, it wouldn't be received well. What if it was an expensive Apple branded toothbrush with all the bells and whistles? Even though their desire can be quenched through the same way, the mouth, it's going to be rejected. Your generosity won't be reciprocated because they currently have no desire for the gift. Give people what they want, and they'll feel indebted to you.

3. You Will Reap a Greater Proportion to the Amount of Seed Sown

If you plant an apple seed, you do not just get an apple seed back, but multiples of fruit with multiples of seed in it. If you participate in sinful behavior you will reap a sinful habit that will be controlling. The harvest is always more than what was sown.

Not all seed will grow, and for different reasons. Some seed is no good. It can't be stored for too long. Some seed will be eaten by birds or other animals. Other seed will fall outside of the ploughed area. Some seed will be in shallow soil and not have enough room for roots to spread. Some seed will grow but be destroyed by natural causes. We can't expect all that we invest to come back to us in a harvest. We should be generous in sowing and know that some seed will take and some won't.

4. You Will Reap After a Period of Endurance

You sow and reap in different seasons. The harvest doesn't come immediately after sowing. Usually, there's a time of growing before you'll see the harvest. You plant the seed, then you have to wait for the seed to "mature". You might have to wait until your good deed for someone comes back to remembrance. They may only refer you to others when they're in conversation about your area of expertise, or they may be in the middle of a boasting competition when they share about the amazing deal you gave them.

To get your good harvest you will need to persevere. To get a bad harvest you don't need to do anything. Weeds will grow whether or not you do anything. An orchard needs to be maintained otherwise it will become full of weeds and the harvest will be poor.

5. You Will Reap of the Same Kind that was Sown

With seed, you receive back the same kind of seed that you have sown. For example, if you sow tomatoes, you aren't going to get back lemons, you'll get tomatoes, hopefully good ones. If you don't listen to people, they will generally not listen to you. If you yell at people you will get back aggression. Whatever it is you sow you will receive back the same kind that you sow.

Imagine a mechanic that does more than expected and fixes something for free. Now obviously the recipient isn't going to do a service on the mechanic's car to show their appreciation. But the recipient would be happy and might become a regular customer or refer them to others. This is the fruit of the initial seed given. In some cases, you might get back other things not directly related to the seed. My dad is an example of that mechanic I have referred to. People would give him things such as smoked fish from a catch the day before. Obviously, the gift was not the same kind of seed, but he received back something that was of value. This was in addition to the fruit of becoming a regular customer and referring others.

6. You Will Reap Only If there Has Been Sowing

If there has been no sowing, there will be no reaping. If the farmer withholds the seed he has in his possession there will be no harvest. It is only in giving away something of value can you get back something of greater value.

Sometimes we can reap where others have sown. It doesn't matter who has sown. For an example, parents often leave an inheritance for their children that help them financially in the years ahead. However if the parents didn't plan to leave anything to their children, there might not be anything left to give, or the parents could pass debt to their children. Whatever was sown or not sown by the parents affected the children.

And another thing: The examples I have given all have a giver and a recipient, with the recipient giving back to the giver, but it doesn't always have to be like that. What might blow your mind is that you could receive back from somewhere or someone different than the one you gave to. This doesn't make sense. Science won't confirm this because it can't measure all the variables you have to take into account. And it's not exactly able to be replicated the same way every time. We have experienced this numerous times with our monetary giving. We found three we could track back that came to exactly ten times the original amount that was given. We had given to someone and received back from somewhere else. I'm not sure why it was ten times the amount given. I would find it difficult to explain in this book why we considered the giving and receiving related. I can't guarantee that it will happen exactly like that again, but as you give under the conditions above and experience this for yourself, you will be amazed to see this law at work.

Give Till It Hurts?

Maybe you've heard of this phrase. It basically means that whatever you give ought to stretch and challenge you. It follows the law of sowing and reaping in that you need to sow generously to be sure to gain the harvest. Yet giving shouldn't be done for the prime motivation of getting your harvest. I mean you could and it would work, but it reveals greed. A giver ought to have a motivation of making a difference to that person or organization. You should be giving without the feeling of regret or coercion.

I remember giving money to someone in need. We were happy to give it. When they needed more money, they came to us first. This time they asked if we could lend them the money. They said that we were the only ones they could think of to help them. What about their other friends or family? They had plenty of them, but they didn't want to lose face with them whereas we already knew their situation. It was the easy option. But it changed our relationship from friends to lender and debtor. Like it or not, it changes things. You might look at their social posts and wonder if they needed to go to a fancy restaurant and spend all that money. Until the debt is paid, it remains tense. It's almost better to have just given the money rather than have a debt outstanding. I would much rather give without expecting anything back.

I was talking to someone the other day at a university. They thought that people should give everything away to the poor, or at least do something to help the poor. Well, I agree with that bit. But how is giving everything away going to help the poor? It might help for a time, but if their mindset hasn't changed, they'll become poor again. The person who gave them the money will be poor as well. Obviously, unforeseen circumstances happen and we can all find ourselves poor one day. Giving isn't limited to money. Sometimes it's better to teach people about how money works and how to get out of poverty. Wealth inequality is real, but we aren't stewards over everybody's lives, just our own.

The Antithesis of a Consumer

Being a giver is the antithesis of being a consumer. It's not that the consumer doesn't give. It's more that the motivation for the consumer to give is self-seeking. A consumer daydreams in order to fulfill selfish desires, whereas a giver wants to fulfill a vision beyond themselves in order to help others. A consumer wants to keep what they have to spend on themselves. A giver wants to save so that when the opportunity arises they can give to help others with their needs. A consumer lusts for more. A giver is content with what they have.

Serve First

Sometimes we can get so caught up in our own lives, we neglect or can't see our part in the grand scheme of things. If people see our actions as being selfish, then whatever we do will be tarnished by their perception. It'll be like we're speaking to the wind and we won't carry any influence in their lives. It's very hard to gain people's trust, but easy to lose it. Also it's impossible to gain it back. Okay, it's not impossible, but I wanted to say that for dramatic effect. It's extremely difficult.

So, how do you overcome this? By genuinely having the best interests of other people in mind. When you deal with others, you should always think the best and not look to hinder or take advantage of them. It can be difficult to have people's best interests in mind and even more difficult to measure. Now, it doesn't mean neglecting yourself or your responsibilities. But it could mean we won't get what we expect, be it a financial, social or another kind of reward.

We should see ourselves as servants looking to help others achieve their potential. In doing this, it helps us see our own potential. In serving with your talents, time, resources and energies, you provide a model for others. What is more, because you give to others, they'll be more likely to follow your leadership. If we motivate, help or encourage others, they'll feel like returning in kind. This happens naturally as people see our motives are pure by us looking out for them.

There are some dodgy practices happening in the internet marketplace. You can see those who aren't genuine a mile off. They don't care about the customer they're ripping off. They're only interested in grabbing your money to get themselves ahead. And it's not the only marketplace like this.

Now, what would happen if you were in a marketplace where you had an audience you treated with respect? You might find they give you the authority to speak into their lives. People won't say this openly, but they'll show you by their actions. For example, if you think a product will help people achieve what they want, then they might buy based on your recommendation. If you're giving them advice, then they might implement your advice. You have a powerful influence over those people, which shouldn't be underestimated or abused. If you understand this principle here, you won't have any problem in becoming wealthy. Well okay, common sense and wisdom help as well.

Conclusion

You can take this knowledge and use it to gain wealth to spend on your desires. But let me warn you now, even if you achieve that which you believe you desire, in the end, you'll feel empty. You're meant to do something important. It's not complicated. You will have to make sacrifices and work hard. But you'll be fulfilled and have a sense of accomplishment rather than the emptiness that so many feel because they don't know what they're meant to do. If we have a vision and deal with our selfish consumerism, it gives us a firm foundation to start with. We can build something of value and find our part to play in helping others.

And so, to recap, here are the six steps of the finance liberation model we have covered in the book:

First, **become a visionary** and discover and start to fulfill your purpose.

Second, *stop being a consumer* who is controlled by their desires.

Third, *become a producer* who has vision and passion for adding value to the marketplace..

Fourth, *become a marketer* who can convince others to the desired outcome.

Fifth, *become an investor* who wisely invests that which they have gained to gain more.

Sixth, *become a giver* who helps others and multiplies that which was sown.

My Gift To You

I want to help you to achieve your own personal finance liberation. As a thank you for reading this book I would like to give you a gift. Please go to the following page:

www.financeliberation.com/gift

Here you will receive any updated information about the book. And I will send you more information about what you can do to achieve finance liberation. It's not to promote things to buy but provide information that will help you on your journey.

Addendum: Save Yourself Rich

I wanted to close with some practical suggestions for saving money. Although, as mentioned in the book, saving won't make you rich, it'll help you with discipline in making wise investment decisions. It can also help to simplify and bring contentment in your life by cutting out those things that can be a weight to you. Some might be a revelation, others might be a little obvious, but if you can improve in a few areas you'll be surprised how it can add up to significant amounts every year. Every bit you save is a bit you can leverage for building wealth. You might be concerned that you won't be able to have any fun if you follow some of the advice. Hey, I don't wish to deny anyone their fun. Trust me, if you can focus on the big picture of finance liberation, then you'll understand the sacrifice is worth it.

A. Clothing

Special Occasions

Do you need those shoes simply because they're on such a great special now? Most people only wear a few clothes out of their wardrobe. The rest just hangs there looking pretty. So, when you buy, make sure that you're actually going to wear what you buy, and more than once. Make sure it's in your color range and that it goes with other clothes that you already have. Don't go buying something for that special occasion because more often than not the special occasion never comes. It might come someday, but when that day comes you might be too fat or have lost a few too many spare tires to fit it. Or you may have totally forgotten about it!

Labels/Brands

Sometimes you might get something of good quality that will last a long time when you buy a branded item. Generally though, will a pair of Levis last you any longer than a budget brand of jeans? Maybe, maybe not, but look at the difference in price. Let's say the Levis are $100 and the no-name brand is $20. Do the Levis last five times longer? No. Do they look better? Maybe. Will anyone notice? Probably not. So, you need to weigh up the ROI. Generally, people buy brands for selfish reasons. To be wealthy and to stay that way you will need to eliminate that as much as you can. I am talking about the finance liberation way of becoming wealthy. Anyone can do this, as opposed to the other ways that require a lot of hard work and are for the lucky few.

Never Pay Retail

When you do buy, buy things you need on sale. Never pay retail prices. Buy out of season. If you wait for the stock clearance at the end of the season, you will get some good deals. For example, at the end of summer, there are sales on shorts because the shops want to move stock during winter promotions. It does mean that you might have to wait a while before you actually use the shorts, but that is planning ahead.

B. Technology

Refurbished Products
Buy refurbished to get big discounts. Refurbished means that there was something wrong with the product, but it has been fixed. Usually you won't experience any issues.

Delayed Gratification
Don't buy the first generation of a product. Generally, they're too expensive and can have a lot of issues. The people who buy the first generation are like beta testers for the new product. They're the ones that pay too much and have to deal with all the issues and bugs.

Buy What You Need, Not What You Want
Do you need the latest 10 GHz processor, or will a 2GHz be sufficient for your needs?

Don't Buy the Brand, Buy the Features
Many companies spend large amounts of money on advertising. That means they'll have to charge more for their products to make a profit.

C. Power Savings

Dishwasher
Use only for heavy loads as you usually have to rinse dishes anyway, so sometimes you won't save much time.

Washing Machine
You don't need hot water washes unless you've got a particularly nasty mess on your hands after a bout of sickness. It doesn't make much difference in cleaning and costs way more.

Oven
If you use your oven for dinner, why not pop in a tray of baking as well? It wastes a lot of power to heat an oven, so maximise it.

Dryer
You don't need it in a lot of environments. These are also very costly to run.

Heater or Air Conditioning
Use sparingly, and only to get the chill off or warm up the air. Wrap up in winter and use airflow in summer.

Showers
Keep to under 5 minutes. If you need much longer, you should be more efficient.

Lights
Turn them off when not in the room. Use energy efficient light bulbs where you can.

Savings in these areas can get your bill down by around five times. For example, we had a similar sized family whose bill was around $400-$500 per month on electricity. At the same time, our bill was around $120 per month.

D. Cleaning

Throw away all your chemical cleaning products. Well, maybe don't throw them away, but certainly, don't buy more. Here is what you can use for all your cleaning: vinegar and baking soda. They're natural, non-allergenic, good for you and the environment. They're also crazy cheap.

E. Food Savings

Grocery

Apart from essentials (I mean things you really need), only buy when on special or in season. Buy in bulk when on special.

Convenience

Do you buy lunch every day? Maybe you should get organized and make it at home. Put yourself on a budget and plan for the times you go out to eat with your colleagues. Don't buy a soft drink. This is where they make a ton of money. It costs them hardly anything for the syrup, and then they carbonate it. Paying for a drink is a waste of money. Just do without that sugar water and bring your own. Nutrition aside, do you really need that $15 combo from that fast food restaurant, or could you buy a couple of items from the loose change menu that would fill you up and that would be enough? You could get 3 x $2 burgers and be fuller than the $15 meal. Or is it about image for you and not about the "food"? Instead of having dessert at a restaurant, why not pick up a yummy treat from the supermarket. You could eat it by the beach or at a look-out spot. Convenience is expensive and sometimes can take longer than cooking for yourself. You can be paying more for a convenient meal than what it can cost you to make it yourself. Also, most of those convenience meals are pumped full of stuff that isn't all that healthy for you.

Kids Meals

Kids are smart, for sure. But kids will get used to whatever you set before them as the norm for their expectations. If you go in and buy them a happy meal, they will expect that every time. Then, if they don't get it, they will be very disappointed. However, if you go in and buy only an ice cream right from the start, then every time they will expect only an ice cream. If you buy something else another time they will be very happy, but they will expect the ice cream as well. They're creatures of habit (like us). We usually buy them a hamburger from the $2 range. Do they complain and point to what the other kids are having? No, they enjoy it and then go play on the playground. It's all about what you set as the expectations. So, as a family of six (now seven), we would spend around $12 where others might spend around $50 at the same place. Are we full and satisfied? No, we aren't exactly bursting at the seams. But it's a stop gap pleasure until we get to the next place.

Romance

We would spend a bit more when we go out by ourselves and not with the kids, but we would always try to get a bargain. Here's the thing: You may have an amazing dining experience and taste sensation for $150, but are your taste-buds going to remember the next day what you ate and is it that much better than the $30 meal? Okay, it probably is. I am not saying that you should not treat yourself every now and then, but is you're every now and then every week? In the end, the food that you put in is fuel for your body, it breaks down to nothing important. Yes, the atmosphere is nice, but it's more important to have people you love with you. See it for what it is, an indulgence. Is it wrong? No. But it's sucking your money up. Calculate the ROI on it and see if it's worth it.

Coffee

What is it with people and coffee? I know there are people, like me, who don't drink it. But for others, it's a must-have ritual fixed into their daily routine. I get it if you are addicted to something you need, to get that fix otherwise you'll get withdrawal symptoms, but again we need to calculate the ROI here and see what we're actually getting for that $4. A temporary high that will lead to a long-term low? A feeling of being cool? Really? And leftovers that go down the bowl. It might be worth the first $4 hit but is it worth all the others? Have you calculated what it's costing per year? A quick calculation of one coffee per day would be around $1,500 per year. Not to mention the addiction that hangs over you. Maybe if you need it, get a coffee maker and make it at home.

F. Entertainment

Movies

I don't go to the movies unless it's something that I have to see that I know will be especially good on the big screen. It can get pretty expensive if you decide you want to buy something to eat while watching a movie as well. Rent it later, when it has finished its status as a New Release. Yes, you can wait. It's called discipline. Some places you can get a weekly movie for $1. It makes for cheap entertainment. Some on-demand internet streaming services are also free if you have a good internet plan. Our local library has a good selection of movies that you can borrow for free.

G. Exercise

Gym

Gym memberships cost a lot of money and many people lose interest long before the membership is up. Ask yourself why you need it. If it's social, then you could become part of a sports team instead. They usually have low subscription fees and train often. Or what about a morning workout group? Other alternatives could be walking or cycling, especially if it's going to save you money on travel.

H. Vehicle

Don't Buy New

You can lose up to 20% of the value as soon as you drive it off the yard. Buy what you can afford. If you don't have any or much money, you can't afford it. So, don't buy it. Use another form of transport to get around. I recently purchased a bike (that is a whole story in itself). The reason I got the bike was to save on transport costs. It also has the added benefit of exercise. But the main reason was to save money. Why not, right? I worked it out that by the time I drive somewhere, try to find a park and then walk to where I need to go, it would be quicker to ride. So, there you go, I'm saving time as well.

Don't Put a Vehicle on Finance

You'll pay way more for the vehicle than the advertised price. Work out exactly how much you would pay over the period of the loan and you would be shocked how much you could overpay.

Purchase a Vehicle for Free

What do I mean by that? Well, you can purchase a vehicle near its lowest point, the point where it will not depreciate much more. Depreciation happens to all material things. They get old and lose value. Houses lose value over time, yet land value rises. If you buy a vehicle for $2,000, when you come to sell it say two years later, you might get around the same amount of money you paid for it. Here is how it works. A vehicle is worth $25,000 brand new and loses 20% straight away. That means it's now $20,000 the minute you drive it off the yard. In 5 years it's now worth $12,000. 10 years $7,000, 15 years $3,500, 20 years $2,000 and it will stay that price until it dies. I am not saying buy something that will fall apart, but you can buy older vehicles that have been well looked after, still look good and run smoothly.

I. Insurance

Some people seem to have insurance for everything and in fact are way over insured. We've never had any major incidents, but the small ones usually cost less if we fix it ourselves than the excess payment with insurance. You should calculate the ROI. What is the percentage likelihood that something is going to happen and what is the cost of that thing happening? In many areas, we don't have insurance. You could put aside the equivalent of your "monthly premiums" into a separate bank account. That could accumulate into enough to cover your incident - and if you don't have any, the money is still yours!

Vehicle Insurance
Unless you are wealthy or need an expensive car for your work, you should see your vehicle as a personal expense, so you should purchase a vehicle that is well within your budget and would be cheap to replace if needed. If you do that, getting full insurance on it wouldn't be necessary. You would only need third party if you damaged someone else's vehicle. If

your vehicle is written off in the process do without until you have saved up to buy another one.

Household Insurance

Usually a waste of money. You should probably only have household assets that would add up to around $20,000. So, don't waste money on this.

Life Insurance

It's good to have for the main money earner, but don't over insure for this, as this is usually to cover funeral costs. Money that you save and don't touch would be better.

Roadside Assist

Some people get this kind of insurance on the off chance that something might happen to their car. Well, the thing with these schemes is that you can usually sign up on the spot, and although it might be a little more expensive to do it that way than being a member, it will save you years of fees.

J. Accommodation

Rent

Depending on your stage of life you can save a lot on rent if it's split with other tenants. You could take on a boarder or an international homestay. If you have the option to stay with family, you can save plenty of money. If you can run any aspect of a business from home, then you can claim those expenses that are used for the business.

House Sitting

Some people actually do this as some sort of business and get all their expenses paid for. I house sat for a period of around six months for two different families, and it saved me a lot of money.

K. Mortgage

The usual advice when getting a mortgage is to pay it off as soon as you can. If you delay paying it off you could end up paying hundreds of thousands more. However, there are some reasons that you might not want to pay it off earlier.

Before you purchase a property, plan out what your intentions are for it. If it's a rental property, then you are going for rental returns and capital growth. If it's a personal home, then you are going to be saving on paying rent to a landlord and getting capital growth. Whatever your strategy, you want to end up paying as little money as you can toward the mortgage. For a rental, obviously, the tenant will be paying. But make sure, that they're covering all the expenses also. In purchasing your own home consider a larger one in which you can take in boarders to help offset the mortgage. If you're still going to be paying more to buy than to rent then consider renting for a time until prices come down. Believe me, they do.

ABOUT THE AUTHOR

After owning and operating businesses in software, furniture, English training and real estate, Dave retired at age 40. He realized that he and his wife, Kim, had more than enough to survive and thrive. They have lived in many countries with a primary goal of starting churches and groups that help communities. Dave, Kim and their five children Hannah, Andrew, Jonathan, Jessica and Emily, currently live in Australia. They continue to support churches and missions throughout the South Pacific.

www.ingramcontent.com/pod-product-compliance
Lightning Source LLC
Chambersburg PA
CBHW071504220526
45472CB00003B/911